P9-CRV-990

designing
for interaction

Creating Smart Applications
and Clever Devices

AIGA

Dan Saffer

New
Riders

Designing for Interaction: Creating Smart Applications and Clever Devices
Dan Saffer

New Riders
1249 Eighth Street
Berkeley, CA 94710
510/524-2178
800/293-9444
510/524-2221 (fax)

Published in association with AIGA Design Press

Find us on the Web at www.newriders.com
To report errors, please send a note to errata@peachpit.com

New Riders is an imprint of Peachpit, a division of Pearson Education

Copyright © 2007 by Daniel Saffer

Acquisitions Editor: Michael Nolan
Project Editors: Cary Norsworthy, Ted Waitt
Development Editor: Judy Ziajka
Production Editor: Becky Winter
Compositor: Maureen Forys, Happenstance Type-O-Rama
Indexer: James Minkin
Proofreader: Dustin Hannum
Cover Design: Mimi Heft
Interior Design: Andrei Pasternak with Maureen Forys

ISBN 0-321-43206-1
9 8 7 6 5 4 3
Printed and bound in the United States of America

Photo Credits

Chapter 1
Figure 1.1 courtesy of SixApart and Mathilde Pignol.
Figure 1.3 courtesy of Cheryl Gach.
Figure 1.4 iStockphoto.
Figure 1.5 iStockphoto.
Figure 1.6 iStockphoto.
Figure 1.8 iStockphoto.
Figure 1.11 iStockphoto.
Case study images courtesy of Corel.
Interview photo courtesy of Marc Rettig.

Chapter 2
Figure 2.1 iStockphoto.
Figure 2.2 iStockphoto.
Figure 2.4 iStockphoto.
Figure 2.5 courtesy of Apple Computer, Inc.
Interview photo courtesy of Thomas Hobbs.

Chapter 3
Figure 3.1 iStockphoto.
Figure 3.2 iStockphoto.
Figure 3.3 iStockphoto.
Figure 3.4 iStockphoto.
Figure 3.5 iStockphoto.
Figure 3.6 iStockphoto.
Figure 3.7 iStockphoto.
Figure 3.8 iStockphoto.
Figure 3.13 iStockphoto.
Figure 3.14 iStockphoto.
Interview photo courtesy of Larry Tesler.

Chapter 4
Figure 4.6 Cartoon by Sidney Harris. © 2003 The New Yorker
  Collection from cartoonbank.com
Interview photo courtesy of Bill Moggridge.

Chapter 5
Figure 5.10 courtesy of Jennifer Anderson, Chun-Yi Chen,
  Phi-Hong Ha, and Dan Saffer.
Figure 5.16 courtesy of Chun-Yi Chen.
Interview photo courtesy of Robert Reimann.

Chapter 6
Figure 6.29 courtesy of Kerry Bodine.
Figure 6.30 courtesy of Daniel Rosen.
Interview photo courtesy of Luke Wroblewski.
Case study images courtesy of Google.

Chapter 7
Figure 7.1 courtesy of BBCi.
Figure 7.5 courtesy of Jan Chipchase.
Figure 7.8 courtesy of Collin Allen.
Figure 7.11 courtesy of Ambient Devices.
Case study images courtesy of Greyworld.
Interview image courtesy of Celia Romaniuk.

Chapter 8
Figure 8.1 courtesy of Antenna Design New York.
Figure 8.2 iStockphoto.
Figure 8.4 iStockPhoto.
Figure 8.5 iStockphoto.
Figure 8.9 courtesy of Rachel M. Murray.
Figure 8.11 courtesy of MAYA.
Figure 8.12 courtesy of Yuan-Chou Chung.
Figure 8.13 courtesy of MAYA.
Figure 8.14 courtesy of Annie Ha, Rosemary Lapka, Jeewon Lee,
  Purin Phanichphant, and Dan Saffer.
Case study images courtesy of Mayo Clinic.
Interview image courtesy of L. Arthi Krishnaswami.

Chapter 9
Figure 9.1 courtesy of Jan Chipchase.
Figure 9.4 courtesy of LEMUR.
Figure 9.7 courtesy of CuteCircuit.
Figure 9.8 courtesy of BodyMedia.
Figure 9.9 courtesy of MySpace and Micki Krimmel.
Case study images courtesy of Mind Candy Design.
Carl DiSalvo photo courtesy of L. Arthi Krishnaswami.
Adam Greenfield photo courtesy of Nurri Kim.

Author photo courtesy of Tim Gasperak and Adaptive Path.

Dedication

For my wife, Rachael, my own Wizard of Oz, who gave me the brains, heart, and courage to undertake this book, and who helps me always return home.

Acknowledgments

The shadow of the two years I spent steeping in design at Carnegie Mellon University looms large over this book. As I wrote, I found myself constantly referring to my notes from that time and hearing the echoes of my professors' words, including those of Dan Boyarski, Kristen Hughes, Karen Moyer, and Jodi Forlizzi. I want to particularly note the influence of Dick Buchanan, who immeasurably broadened my understanding of this discipline, and my friend and advisor Shelley Evenson, who taught me at least half of what I know about interaction design. Without her knowledge and experience, poorly filtered through me, this book would be shallow indeed.

My interviewees were generous with their time and expertise, and I'd like to especially thank them. Your presence in my book honors me. A tip of the hat to Peter Merholz for the excellent suggestion.

The case studies, too, greatly improved this book, providing grounding for some of the big concepts. For their contributions, I'd like to thank Jennifer Fraser and Jessica Gould at Corel, Chad Thornton at Google, Maureen Wegner at Mayo, Andrew Shoben at Greyworld, and Michael Smith at Mind Candy Design. Thanks, too, to Katie Linder for her help in tracking these down.

I'm also grateful to companies who lent their beautiful product images to the book, illustrating my points better than I could have with words alone.

The staff at Peachpit/New Riders has been a tremendous help in making this book what it is, guiding me (sometimes dragging me) to make it better, and the book is much improved for it. My editors Cary Norsworthy, Michael Nolan, Ted Waitt, Becky Winter, and especially Judy Ziajka have polished my rough edges (and there were many) into the fine tome you have in your hands (or on your screen). Another special thanks goes to my friend and technical editor Phi-Hong Ha, who never hesitated to tell me I was wrong or that I could do better.

My colleagues at Adaptive Path have been generous with their patience and my schedule, not to mention my salary, which has allowed me to tackle this challenge. A special shout out to Jesse James Garrett who introduced me to New Riders.

Thanks to my parents, who bought me my first computer (a Timex Sinclair 2068) and a 300-baud modem and who paid the ensuing long-distance phone bills.

My daughter endured my frequent distractions and even-more-frequent grumpiness. Fiona, I'm sorry. There's now more time for Hello Kitty Uno and Princess Monopoly.

Last, and most important, without the support of my wife, Rachael King, the creation of this book would have been impossible. She convinced me I could do it, encouraged me when I faltered, and gave me the time to complete it. This book is as much a product of her generosity as it is of my words.

Contents

Chapter 6: Interface Design Basics   121

Chapter 7: Smart Applications and Clever Devices   151

About the Author

Although he wouldn't hear the term "interaction design" for another decade and a half, Dan Saffer did his first interaction design work in 1985 at the age of 15 when he designed and ran a dial-up game on his Apple IIe, a 2600-baud modem, two floppy drives, and a phone line. And yes, it was in his parents' basement.

Since then, he's worked formally in interactive media since 1995 as a web-master, information architect, copywriter, developer, producer, creative lead, and interaction designer. Currently, he is an interaction designer at the design firm Adaptive Path.

Dan has designed a wide range of projects, from Web sites and interactive television services to mobile devices and robot navigation systems. His clients have included Fortune 500 companies, government agencies, non-profits, and start-ups. He holds a Master of Design in Interaction Design from Carnegie Mellon University, where he taught interaction design fundamentals.

A member of AIGA and the Industrial Designers Society of America (IDSA), he also sits on the board of the Interaction Design Association (IxDA).

Dan lives in San Francisco and can be found online at www.odannyboy.com.

We become what we behold. We shape our tools, and thereafter our tools shape us.

—Marshall McLuhan

Introduction

On the morning of September 11, 2001, I was less than a mile from the smoking towers of the World Trade Center. As I walked dazed through the surreal streets of lower Manhattan, I saw powerful scenes of connection and interaction. People had pulled TVs out from their apartments onto the streets, and crowds were gathered around them. Commuters frantically called home from their mobile phones. An intricate web of systems coordinated firefighters, police, and emergency medical technicians, who rushed to the terrible scene, sirens wailing down the avenues. At my office in SoHo, friends contacted me via instant messenger, wanting to know if I was okay. Since my phone was only sporadically working, I coordinated my eventual flight to Brooklyn through e-mail with a friend.

This is a book about design, a particular type of design called *interaction design*. It's a new discipline, even though humans have been using interaction design since before recorded history. Interaction design is about *people*: how people connect with other people through the products and services they use. Interaction designers create these products and services—those we rely on in times of crisis like September 11th, and those we enjoy in quiet, joyful moments.

Whether you're an interaction designer already or just interested in interaction design, even if you don't know (yet) what that really means, this book is for you. I hope it contains information of interest to novices and experts alike, starting with the questions "What is an interaction?" and "What is interaction design?" and ending with a look into the future of interaction design. My goal in writing this book is to make your understanding of interaction design richer, deeper, and broader.

A disclaimer before we begin: Interaction design is a new field, and it usually takes decades before any field has firm footing. This book is a stake in the ground—what I've found to be right and true. I hope, either while reading or (even better) when practicing interaction design, you discover what I've recorded here to be true as well.

San Francisco
March 2006

Notes on Nomenclature

Throughout this book, I have had to use the unfortunate, yet standard, term *user* to designate the human beings who use (or will use) the products and services discussed in this book. I am no fan of this term. As has been noted elsewhere, only in drug trafficking are there also "users," albeit of a different sort. But I could not find a better term that wasn't incredibly clunky, so *user* the term remained.

I am also noting that the term *computer* has definitely reached the end of its usefulness. I have tried, when and where appropriate, to use the terms *digital device* or *microprocessor* instead.

the professional association for design

164 Fifth Avenue
New York, NY 10010
Tel 212 807 1990
Fax 212 807 1799
www.aiga.org

There has been no more fundamental and revolutionary transformation over the past two decades than the invitation for ordinary people to influence and design their own experiences. Although this change has occurred as a result of technology, hardware and software are merely the tools. The real transformation has been in the way designers have approached the role of every person in the design of an experience, an interaction with other people, ideas and objects.

Dan Saffer provides us with a fresh, accessible and thoughtful guide to interaction design—a concept just being defined—in *Designing for Interaction*. It is a book that should fast become a standard reference in the process of design thinking for purposeful interactions.

AIGA copublishes selected works by thought leaders in design—authors whose works define new boundaries of design or support practicing designers in their quest for expanding dimensions of excellence and relevance. *Designing for Interaction* has set the stake in the ground for interaction design.

Richard Grefé
Executive director, AIGA

The AIGA Design Press is committed to stimulating thinking at the intersection of design, business and culture. The Press is a partnership with New Riders Publishing as a means of extending AIGA's traditional role in advancing the art, practice and theory of design. With rigor and enthusiasm, The Press will embrace new fields, uncover powerful modes of inquiry and pursue excellence in design thinking. AIGA is the oldest and largest professional association of designers in the United States. Its members include all disciplines involved in the process of designing.

1

What Is Interaction Design?

Every moment of every day, millions of people send e-mail, talk on mobile phones, instant message each other, record TV shows with TiVo, and listen to music on their iPods. All of these things are made possible by good engineering. But it's interaction design that makes them usable, useful, and fun.

You benefit from good interaction design every time you:

▶   Go to an automatic teller machine (ATM) and withdraw cash in a few simple touches on a screen.

▶   Become engrossed in a computer game.

▶   Share photos on the Web.

▶   Text message a friend from your mobile phone.

▶   Are treated quickly and well in an emergency room.

▶   Post to your blog (**Figure 1.1**).

Figure 1.1

Blogging tool
LiveJournal enables
one-to-many
interactions.

But the reverse is often also true. We suffer from poor interaction design all around us. Thousands of interaction design problems wait to be solved—such as when you:

▶ Try to use self-checkout at a grocery store and it takes you half an hour.

▶ Can't get your car to tell you what's wrong with it when it breaks down.

▶ Wait at a bus stop with no idea when the next bus will arrive.

▶ Struggle to synchronize your mobile phone to your computer.

▶ Stand in line for hours at the Department of Motor Vehicles.

Any time you communicate with people through a device like a mobile phone or computer or through a service like the DMV, interaction designers could be involved. Indeed, for the best experience, they *should* be involved.

Back in 1990, Bill Moggridge, a principal of the design firm IDEO, realized that for some time he and some of his colleagues had been creating a very different kind of design. It wasn't product design exactly, but they were definitely designing products. Nor was it communication design, although they used some of that discipline's tools as well. It wasn't computer science either, although a lot of it had to do with computers and software. No, this was something different. It drew on all those disciplines, but was something else, and it had to do with connecting people through the products they used. Moggridge called this new practice *interaction design*.

In the years since then, interaction design has grown from a tiny, specialized discipline to one practiced by tens of thousands of people all over the world, many of whom don't call themselves interaction designers and may not even be aware of the discipline. Universities now offer degrees in it, and you'll find practitioners of interaction design at every major software and design firm, as well as in banks such as Wells Fargo, hospitals such as the Mayo Clinic, and appliance manufacturers such as Whirlpool.

The rise of the commercial Internet in the mid 1990s and the widespread incorporation of microprocessors into machines such as cars, dishwashers, and phones where previously they hadn't been used led to this explosive growth in the number of interaction designers because suddenly a multitude of serious interaction problems needed to be solved. Our gadgets became digital, as did our workplaces, homes, transportation, and communication devices. Our everyday stuff temporarily became unfamiliar to us; the confusion we once collectively had about how to set the clock on the VCR spread to our entire lives. We had to relearn how to dial a phone number and work the stereo and use our computers. It was the initial practitioners of interaction design—mostly coming from other disciplines—who helped us begin to make sense of our newly digitized world, and these same people now, aided by new interaction designers, continue to refine and practice the craft as our devices, and our world, grow ever more complex.

What Are Interactions and Interaction Design?

Although we experience examples of good and bad interaction design every day, interaction design as a discipline is tricky to define. In part, this is the result of its interdisciplinary roots: in industrial design, human factors, and human-computer interaction. It's also because a lot of interaction design is invisible, functioning behind the scenes. Why do Windows and Mac OS X, which basically do the same thing and can, with some tinkering, even look identical, *feel* so different? It's because interaction design is about behavior, and behavior is much harder to observe and understand than appearance. It's much easier to notice and discuss a garish color than a subtle transaction that may, over time, drive you crazy.

Interaction design is the art of facilitating interactions between humans through products and services. It is also, to a lesser extent, about the interactions between humans and those products that have some sort of "awareness"—that is, products with a microprocessor that are able to sense and respond to humans. Let's break this definition down.

Interaction design is an art—an applied art, like furniture making; it's not a science. Although best practices have emerged over the past three decades, the discipline has yet to arrive at hard and fast rules that can be proven via scientific methods and that are true in all instances. Interaction design is by its nature contextual: it solves specific problems under a particular set of circumstances. For example, even though a 1994 Mosaic browser (**Figure 1.2**) is an excellent piece of interaction design, you wouldn't install it on your computer now. It served its purpose *for its time and context*.

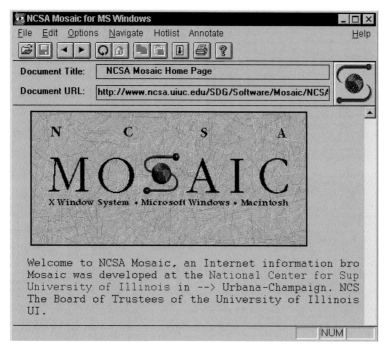

Figure 1.2

The Mosaic browser was a fantastic piece of interaction design...for 1994. You wouldn't use it now.

Like other arts such as painting, interaction design involves many methods and methodologies in its tasks, and ways of working go in and out of vogue and often compete for dominance. Currently, a very user-centered design methodology in which products are researched and tested with users (see Chapter 4) is in style, but this hasn't always been the case, and recently these methods have been challenged (see Chapter 2)—Microsoft performs extensive user testing and research; Apple, known for its innovative interaction design, does none.

Interaction design is an applied art; its usefulness comes in its application to real problems, such as figuring out the best way to send e-mail. Its purpose is to foster communication—an interaction—between two or more human beings or, to a lesser degree, between a human and an artificial entity capable of responding in some manner, such as a computer, mobile phone, or digital appliance. These communications can take many forms; they can be one-on-one as with a telephone call, one-to-many as with a blog, or many-to-many as with the stock market.

When people communicate through or with something—a phone, a blog, the stock market—they need those products and services designed to provide an optimal experience that facilitates interaction. Those products are the rich soil in which interaction design grows, and thanks to the Internet, wireless devices, mobile phones, and a host of other technologies, the soil is richer than ever.

Note that these products do not necessarily involve a computer screen. They can be digital (software) or analog (robots), physical (PDAs) or incorporeal (workflows), or some combination thereof. There are interaction designers (called imagineers) working at Disney theme parks, for instance, who work in all these realms when creating a single attraction. Interaction design talents are also employed to create systems such as the Netflix movie rental service or City CarShare, a service for sharing cars, which involve nondigital components, as we'll discuss in Chapter 8.

Since technology frequently changes, good interaction design doesn't align itself to any one technology or medium in particular. Interaction design should be technologically agnostic, concerned only with the right technologies for the task at hand, be it a complex software application or a simple sign.

Interaction design is concerned with the behavior of products and services, with how products and services *work*. Interaction designers should spend a great deal of time defining these behaviors (see Chapter 5), but they should never forget that the goal is to facilitate interactions between humans. Certainly, many interaction designers work with products that have "awareness"—the ability to sense and respond to human input—such as computers, mobile phones, and many so-called smart environments. But interaction design isn't about interaction with computers (that's the discipline of human-computer interaction) or interaction with machines (that's industrial design). It's about making connections between people *through* these products, not connecting to the product itself.

Why Interaction *Design*?

The term *design* can be difficult to get a handle on. Consider this infamous sentence by design history scholar John Heskett: "Design is to design a design to produce a design."

People have many preconceived notions about design, not the least of which is that design concerns only how things look: design as decoration or styling. But communication (graphic) and industrial design also bring ways of working that interaction designers should embrace. Here are some of the attitudes that designers have:

▸ **Focusing on users.** Designers know that users don't understand or care how the company that makes a product is run and structured. Users care about doing their tasks and achieving their goals within their limits. Designers are advocates for end-users.

▸ **Finding alternatives.** Designing isn't about choosing among multiple options—it's about creating options, finding a "third option" instead of choosing between two undesirable ones. This creation of multiple possible solutions to problems sets designers apart. Consider, for example, Google's AdWords. The company needed advertising for revenue, but users hated traditional banner ads. Thus, designers came up with a third approach: text ads.

▸ **Using ideation and prototyping.** Designers find their solutions through brainstorming and then, most important, building models to test the solutions (**Figure 1.3**). Certainly, scientists and architects

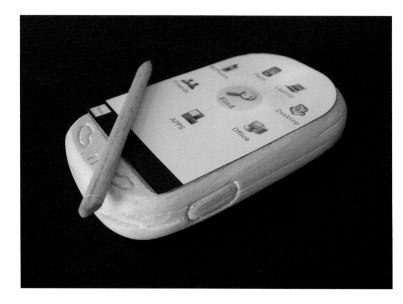

Figure 1.3

Designers create prototypes to find a solution, not *the* solution.

and even accountants model things, but design involves a significant difference: design prototypes aren't fixed. Any particular prototype doesn't necessarily represent *the* solution, only *a* solution. It's not uncommon to use several prototypes to create a single product. Jeff Hawkins, designer of the original Palm Pilot, famously carried around small blocks of wood until he came upon the right size, shape, and weight for the device.

▸ **Collaborating and addressing constraints.** Few designers work alone. Designers usually need resources (money, materials, developers, printers, and so on) to produce what they dream up, and these resources come with their own constraints. Designers seldom have carte blanche to do whatever they want. They must address business goals, compromise with teammates, and meet deadlines. Designing is almost always a team effort.

▸ **Creating appropriate solutions.** Most designers create solutions that are appropriate only to a particular project at a particular point in time. Designers certainly carry experience and wisdom from one project to the next, but the ultimate solution should uniquely address the issues of that particular problem. This is not to say that the solution (the product) cannot be used in other contexts—experience tells us it can and will be—but that the same exact solution cannot (or shouldn't anyway) be exactly copied for other projects. Amazon has a great e-commerce model, but it can't be exactly replicated elsewhere (although pieces of it certainly can be); it works well within the context of the Amazon site. Design solutions have to be appropriate to the situation.

▸ **Drawing on a wide range of influences.** Because design touches on so many subject areas (psychology, ergonomics, economics, engineering, architecture, art, and more), designers bring to the table a broad, multidisciplinary spectrum of ideas from which to draw inspiration and solutions.

▸ **Incorporating emotion.** In analytical thinking, emotion is seen as an impediment to logic and making the right choices. In design, products without an emotional component are lifeless and do not connect with people. Emotion needs to be thoughtfully included in design decisions. What would the Volkswagen Beetle be without whimsy?

Because interaction designers employ these approaches and the qualitative methods and the processes that other design disciplines use (see Chapters 2, 4, and 5), interaction design's strongest ties are to the discipline of design—not to, say, human-computer interaction or cognitive psychology, although it does draw heavily on those fields. Interaction designers are *designers*, for good and ill.

A (Very) Brief History of Interaction Design

There's a tendency to think that interaction design began around the time that Bill Moggridge named it, in 1990, but that's not really true. Interaction design probably began, although obviously not as a formalized discipline, in prerecorded history, when Native Americans and other tribal peoples used smoke signals to communicate over long distances, and the Celts and Inuit used stone markers called cairns or inukshuk as landmarks, to communicate over time (**Figure 1.4**).

Many centuries later, in the mid 1830s, Samuel Morse created a system to turn simple electromagnetic pulses into a language of sorts and to communicate those words over long distances; over the next 50 years, Morse code

Figure 1.4

A modern cairn. Cairns are products that transmit messages through time.

and the telegraph spread across the globe (**Figure 1.5**). Morse not only invented the telegraph, but also the entire system for using it: everything from the electrical systems, to the mechanism for tapping out the code, to the training of telegraph operators. This didn't happen overnight, naturally, but the telegraph was the first instance of communication technology that, unlike the printing press, was too sophisticated for a small number of people to install and use. It required the creators to design an entire system of use.

Similarly, other mass communication technologies, from the telephone to radio to television, required engineers to design systems of use and interfaces for the new technologies. And these systems and interfaces were needed not only for the receiving devices—the telephones, radios, and television sets—but also for the devices used to create and send messages: the telephone switches, microphones, television cameras, control booths, and so on. All of these components required interaction design, although it certainly wasn't called that at the time.

But the machines that fueled these technologies were, for the most part, just that: machines. They responded to human input certainly, but not in a sophisticated way. They didn't have any awareness that they were being used. For that, we needed computers.

Figure 1.5

Morse code transmitter. The telegraph was the first technology system for communicating over long distances that required complex assembly and training to use.

1940s to 1980s

The first wave of computers—ENIAC and its ilk—were engineered, not designed. Humans had to adapt to using them, not vice versa, and this meant speaking the machines' language, not ours. Entering anything into the computer required hours preparing a statement on punch cards or paper tape for the machine to read; these paper slips were the interface (**Figure 1.6**). Engineers expended very little design effort to make the early computers more usable. Instead, they worked to make them faster and more powerful, so the computers could solve complicated computational problems.

Figure 1.6

Punch cards—the first interface with computers.

Engineers began to focus on people only in the 1960s, when they started to devise new methods of input. Engineers added control panels to the front of computers, allowing input through a complicated series of switches, usually in combination with a set of punch cards that were processed as a group (batch processing). Meanwhile, at labs such as Xerox PARC and universities such as MIT, engineers and designers experimented with monitors for visual output, designed simple games, and explored new interfaces such as the mouse and light pen. Suddenly, many more applications for computers seemed possible, albeit to a small group of people. Visionaries such as Xerox

PARC's Bob Taylor started thinking of computers not as just processing devices, but instead as communication devices. Over the next decade, the focus shifted from the computer itself—the hardware—to the software that runs it.

Designers, programmers, and engineers in the 1970s introduced the command-line interface and such industry-defining software as VisiCalc and WordStar (**Figure 1.7**). Finally, companies started designing computers for people beyond computer scientists and trained operators. This new emphasis came to fruition in the early 1980s with the introduction by Apple Computer of the graphical user interface, first in the Lisa and then in the Macintosh, to a mass audience. Bulletin board systems (BBSs) like The WELL sprung up so that people could leave e-mail and messages for one another on remote computers using dial-up modems.

Figure 1.7

WordStar and its ilk were the first pieces of commercial software that weren't designed by programmers for programmers.

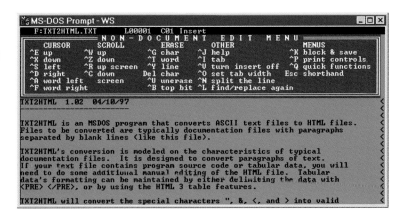

At the same time as these developments were occurring in the computing field, other disciplines that eventually informed interaction design were growing. Engineers and industrial designers such as Henry Dreyfuss created the new field of human factors, which focused on the design of products for different sizes and shapes of people. The field of ergonomics focused on workers' productivity and safety, determining the best ways to perform tasks. Cognitive psychology, focusing on human learning and problem solving, experienced a resurgence, led by such academics as Alan Newell and George Miller.

1990s to the Present

The era of networked computing and of interaction design as a formal discipline began in earnest during the 1990s. The World Wide Web, which allows anyone to easily publish hypertext documents accessible worldwide to anyone with a modem, and the mass adoption of e-mail brought the need for better interaction design to the forefront.

At the same time, engineers and designers began building sensors and microprocessors, which were getting smaller, cheaper, and more powerful, into things that weren't considered computers: cars, appliances, and electronic equipment. Suddenly, these physical objects could demonstrate kinds of behavior that they previously couldn't; they could display an "awareness" of their environment and of how they were being used that was previously inconceivable. Cars could monitor their own engines and alert drivers to problems before they occurred. Stereos could adjust their settings based on the type of music being played. Dishwashers could lengthen their wash cycles depending on how dirty the dishes were. All these behaviors needed to be designed and, most important, communicated to the human beings using the objects.

Other pieces of technology facilitated interactions among people, mostly in the entertainment space. Karaoke spread from bars in China and Japan to the United States (**Figure 1.8**). Arcade video games like Dance Dance Revolution allowed expression in front of crowds. Multiplayer games on computers and game consoles like the Sony Playstation facilitated competition and collaboration in new ways. Online communities like Everquest and The Sims Online incorporated sophisticated economies that rivaled those of offline countries.

Mobile phones and devices, which had existed since the 1980s, enjoyed explosive market growth in the 1990s. Today, billions of customers carry these devices with them. Starting as simply a means of making calls on the go, mobile phones can now contain a myriad of digital features that rival those of desktop computers. Personal digital assistants (PDAs) got off to a shaky start with the failure of Apple's Newton in 1995, but by the end of the decade, they had gained traction with devices like the Palm Pilot and Blackberry PDAs. Computers, too, became mobile devices as laptops entered the market; by 2003 laptops were outselling desktops in the United States.

Figure 1.8

Although the butt of jokes, the karaoke machine is a surprisingly rich example of interaction design. It provides a way to communicate emotionally with friends.

As the Internet matured, so did the technologies creating and driving it. Since the end of the 1990s, the Internet has become less about reading content than about doing things: executing stock trades, making new acquaintances, selling items, manipulating live data, sharing photos, making personal connections between one piece of content and another. The Internet also provides several new ways of communicating, among them instant messaging and Voice over Internet Protocol (VoIP) (**Figure 1.9**). The Internet has become a platform for applications, in much the same way that Microsoft DOS once was, but these applications can take advantage of the many features of the Internet: collective actions like the SETI@home project in which people compete to see who can find extraterrestrial activity first, data that is collected passively from large numbers of people as with Amazon's "People who bought this also bought…" feature,

Figure 1.9

Skype takes a familiar paradigm, the buddy list from instant messaging, and couples it with a new technology, Voice over IP (VoIP), to allow people to make phone calls over the Internet.

far-flung social communities such as Yahoo Groups, aggregation of many sources of data in XML and RSS feeds, near real-time access to timely data like stock quotes and news, and easy sharing of content such as blogs.

But it's not just the Internet—it's also *access* to the Internet, through broadband connections and WiFi wireless networks, that is changing the types of interactions we can have and where we can have them. There's never been a better time to be an interaction designer. The discipline's future contains both many challenges and many possibilities.

Marc Rettig on Interaction Design's History and Future

Marc Rettig is a designer, educator, and researcher, as well as founder and principal of Fit Associates. He has taught at Carnegie Mellon's Graduate School of Design (where he held the 2003 Nierenberg Distinguished Chair of Design) and the Institute of Design, IIT, in Chicago. Marc served as chief experience officer of the user experience firm HannaHodge and was a director of user experience at Cambridge Technology Partners.

When does the history of interaction design begin?

I'll pick the work at Xerox PARC on the Star interface as a very early example of self-conscious interaction design, the publication of which influenced others to begin working in a similar way. As just one example, the idea of associating a program with a picture was born there. We call them icons, and forget what a breakthrough connection between interface element and underlying meaning that once was. That was the early-to-mid 1970s, and the Star papers are still great reading.

What fields have had the greatest influence on interaction design?

As it is currently practiced? Well, software development and graphic design. To some extent, industrial design. A dab of psychology and human factors. A dab of business.

Marc Rettig on Interaction Design's History and Future *Continued*

What I imagine we need more of: filmmaking and theater, biology, counseling and therapy (the professionals at acquiring and checking an empathic point of view), maybe anthropology. And especially linguistics—some new branch of linguistics that nobody is yet carving out: the linguistics of designed interactions.

What can interaction designers learn from noninteractive tools?

I'd like to spin the question slightly by observing that to an interaction designer, watching a tool in use is the same as observing a conversation. Everything, in a sense, has its inputs and outputs. From that point of view, the boundary between "interactive" and "noninteractive" tools starts to dissolve.

Interaction design is largely about the meaning that people assign to things and events, and how people try to express meanings. So to learn from any tool, interactive or not, go watch people using it. You'll hear them talk to the tool. You'll see them assign all sorts of surprising interpretations to shapes, colors, positioning, dings, dents, and behaviors. You'll see them fall in love with a thing as it becomes elegantly worn. You'll see them come to hate a thing and choose to ignore it, sell it, or even smash it. And I guarantee you won't have to do much of this before you encounter someone who makes a mental mapping you would never dream possible. And you'll learn from that.

I've been using tea kettles as an example in some of my teaching, because on the one hand kettles are so familiar to us, and they're only interactive in a borderline, predictable, mechanical sort of way. But once you start to examine the meanings involved with kettles in use, you realize they have things to say that people would love to know, but most designs don't allow them to be said. "I'm getting hot, but I have no water in me." "My water is a good temperature for a child's cocoa." "I'm too hot to touch." "I need to be cleaned." And so on. I'd love the chance to take a serious interaction design approach to something like a tea kettle.

A Stew of Acronyms

Interaction design as a formal discipline has been around for less than two decades. It's a young field, still defining itself and figuring out its place among sister disciplines such as information architecture (IA), industrial design (ID), communication (or graphic) design (CD), user-experience (UX) design, user-interface engineering (UIE), human-computer interaction (HCI), usability engineering (UE), and human factors (HF). In addition, many of these other disciplines are also new and still discovering their boundaries. **Figure 1.10** clarifies the relationships.

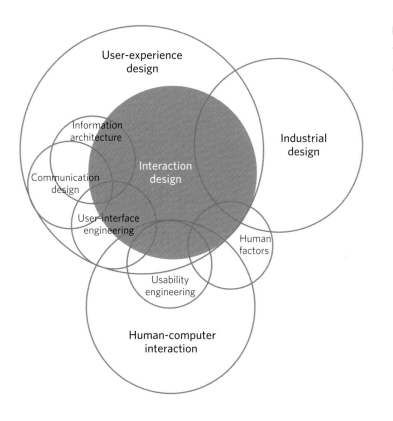

Figure 1.10

The overlapping disciplines of interaction design.

As you can see, most of the disciplines fall at least partially under the umbrella of user-experience design, the discipline of looking at all aspects—visual design, interaction design, sound design, and so on—of the user's encounter with a product or service and making sure they are in harmony.

Information architecture is concerned with the structure of content: how to best structure and label content so that users find the information they need. Yahoo, with its dozens of labeled and categorized content areas, offers an excellent illustration of information architecture. Communication design is about creating a visual language to communicate content. The fonts, colors, and layout of Web sites and printed materials like this book provide examples of communication design. Industrial design is about form—shaping objects in a way that communicates their use while also making them functional. Physical objects like chairs, tables, and refrigerators illustrate industrial design. Human factors makes sure those objects conform to the limitations of the human body, both physically and psychologically. Human-computer interaction is closely related to interaction design, but its methods are more quantitative, and its focus (as its name implies) is strongly on how humans relate to computers, unlike interaction design, which is about how humans relate to each other. The operating system on your computer provides an example of HCI. User-interface engineering is a subset of interaction design and HCI; it focuses on the controls of a digital device (see Chapter 6). Your digital camera's display is an example of UIE. Usability engineering is about testing products to make sure they make sense to users.

It's easy to see why people are confused!

Although these disciplines are separate, as the figure illustrates, they still overlap a great deal. Most successful products, especially digital products, involve multiple disciplines working in harmony. What is a laptop computer except a blend of the fruits of all these disciplines? Separating them is nearly impossible.

Not every organization needs a specialist working in each discipline; within an organization, one person, who might be called anything from an information architect to a user-interface engineer, can—and probably will—work in several, shifting back and forth as needs require. It's the discipline that is important, not the title. The "imagineer" at Disney might do a job similar to that of the "user-interface architect" at a startup company.

Case Study: Corel PowerTRACE

The Company

Corel Corporation, a producer of graphics and office productivity software.

The Problem

CorelDRAW Graphics Suite is popular with sign makers, engravers, printers, and publishers, who often start their work with a low-quality bitmap image (such as from print or the Web) that needs to be converted to high-quality vector format. Once an image has been converted to vector format, it can be resized to any size necessary without any loss of resolution, so making signs or brochures from business card logos or Web logos is much easier. Corel had an application—Corel Trace—to convert bitmap images to vector graphics, but users had many problems with it. For one thing, it was not well integrated with the rest of the graphics suite, and the controls it offered weren't enough to meet users' needs. Some users were even having to redraw bitmap images by hand—a tedious process that could waste hours of time.

The Process

A design prototype from the Corel team shows the work in progress.

Case Study: Corel PowerTRACE *Continued*

The design team at Corel interviewed users and watched how they worked to better understand this tracing part of the user workflow. The Corel software design team then reevaluated the usefulness of Corel Trace as a stand-alone tracing utility and concluded that users would be better served by a different solution: one that was built into the main design software, CorelDRAW.

The Solution

Through iterative design and prototyping, the design team created Corel PowerTRACE, which enables users to preview a trace as a translucent overlay directly on top of the original image, so that users can easily compare before-and-after results. Users no longer have to redraw bitmaps by hand. Corel PowerTRACE allows them much greater control over the tracing, including control over the number of curves and types of colors that appear in the new vector graphic. PowerTRACE also better reflects users' workflow, since it's integrated into CorelDRAW instead of being a stand-alone utility.

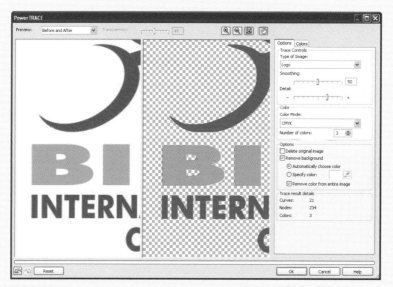

PowerTRACE saves users significant time and effort by providing the tracing control needed for a seamless workflow.

Why Practice Interaction Design?

In poem after poem, the late barfly poet extraordinaire Charles Bukowski noted that it wasn't the big things that drove people mad, it was the small stuff: little things not going well, small irritants that over time made you crazy—the leaking faucet, the stains that won't come out of clothes, the mobile phone that won't dial. Interaction designers try to ameliorate some of that annoyance, making sure that the products and services people deal with make sense, are usable and useful, and are even engaging and fun. Some of what good interaction designers do is make the world better by removing those little irritants in life, some of which we don't know exist until they are gone.

Humans have an amazing tendency to become accustomed to the terrible, inconvenient, and awkward. We can live with horrible situations for long periods until something better comes along, something we may not have even known we needed. Take the telephone, for instance. For decades, all calls had to be routed through a human operator, who (if she or he felt like it) could also listen in on your call (**Figure 1.11**). Dial phones weren't introduced until 1919, and it wasn't until the 1950s—80 years after the phone was invented—that direct distance dialing (DDD) allowed callers to dial long-distance without the help of an operator. The last manual phones weren't phased out until the 1970s—almost a hundred years after they were introduced!

Figure 1.11

Old telephone exchange. Imagine all your long-distance calls being routed through this. Now imagine having to operate it for long periods of time.

But interaction design isn't only about fixing problems; it's also about facilitating interactions between people in richer, deeper, better ways—that is, finding new ways to better connect human beings to one another, and by doing so, make the world a better place to live. The Internet would be a collection of servers and wires without Web browsers, e-mail clients, games, blogging tools, social networking sites, and instant messaging and VoIP programs. These products—these designed products—like the smoke signals and cairns of our ancient ancestors, allow us to connect with one another through time and space. It's easy to forget this in the middle of a harried project, but the work that interaction designers do matters in profound ways. Interaction designers change the world, a little at a time, through the products and services they create.

2

Starting Points

There are few things as professionally daunting to a new interaction designer as starting a project. Projects generally begin for one of two reasons: something is broken or something doesn't exist. "Users are complaining about X!" a business manager will exclaim. "We need to do Y!" (Even though Y might not be the solution, it's the interaction designer's job to figure that out.) Or else someone, somewhere, muses, "Wouldn't it be great if we could do Z?" and, if resources such as money, time, and brain power (that's where interaction designers come in) can be found, the project begins.

But once a project is launched, how does an interaction designer get started? What tools and methods do designers use to come up with solutions? Although many working today insist there's one way—user-centered design (UCD)—to work, this simply isn't true. There are several ways to approach problems, as we'll discuss later in this chapter. But first, let's talk a little about problems themselves.

The Problem with Problems

There's an old joke among software developers. When something works in an unexpected but strangely effective way, the developers often kid, "Oh, that's not a bug. That's a feature." While this is usually only a joke, designers can use the same technique of reframing the problem when tackling their own projects. In fact, there's an old joke among designers: "It's not a problem. It's an opportunity."

Before a designer typically gets involved in a project, a business usually encounters or discovers a problem or a perceived problem. A current product isn't selling or working well or is simply out of style—witness the launch of new mobile phones every six months. Or a competitor has launched a better product, as occurred in the mid 1990s as companies vied to produce the best Internet browser. Or a new market has opened up and products need to be invented for that market, which is what happened when Voice over IP (VoIP) became practical and everything from Web sites to applications to phones needed to be designed. These "problems" become the basis for involving a designer.

Unless the problem is simple and narrowly defined (for instance, users can't find the Submit button at the end of a form), interaction designers shouldn't take any problem at face value. Often, what seems at first glance to be simple, really isn't (and, rarely, vice versa).

Consider the seemingly simple problem of an online form on which users have trouble finding the Submit button at the form's end. The simple solution might be just to move the button to a better place or make the button more prominent through color, size, or shape. But this issue could also be an indicator of a larger problem. Maybe the form is too long. Maybe users don't understand why they are filling out the form, and the problem isn't that they can't find the button, but that they abandon the form in the middle, not caring to finish it. Or maybe they are afraid to click the button because they don't know what will happen next. And so on. Simple problems can be indicators of larger ones.

That being said, while working, interaction designers shouldn't overly complicate things and should *pick their battles*. Sometimes a button problem is just a button problem. Not every project needs to be completely rethought and broken down. The teams that interaction designers work with would hate them if they constantly did that. But—and this will be a theme in this book—be deliberate in the choices you make. If making the button bigger will solve most of the problem, well then, make the button bigger.

But fixing buttons that are too small isn't typically the type of problem that interaction designers are asked to solve. Certainly buttons and controls (see Chapter 6) will often be part of the solution, but the situations that interaction designers typically need to address are much messier. The types of problems that interaction designers often deal with have been called "wicked problems," a term coined in the 1960s by design theorist H. J. Rittel. Wicked problems aren't fully understood and have fuzzy boundaries, they have lots of people (stakeholders) with a say in them, they have lots of constraints, and they have no clear solution. Sounds like fun, right? But these are the sorts of issues that designers, especially interaction designers, tackle all the time. Design is not for the faint hearted.

Defining the Project

Examining the problem shouldn't be a solo activity. As much as designers like to think so, they aren't all knowing and all seeing. Designers need input and other points of view from clients, stakeholders, colleagues, teammates, and others who have maybe thought about this situation (or similar situations). Designers typically get this information from two places: the design brief and stakeholder interviews. (Designers can, of course, get input from users too; see Chapter 4.)

The brief is a document, usually from the client (or an internal business manager or unit hereafter referred to as a client), but it can also be created by the designer from information culled from the stakeholder interviews. It should lay out the reasons for employing the designer (the problem) and often it may make suggestions for the solution as well. The brief is an excellent starting point for gathering information. Briefs can contain such information as brand considerations, technical constraints, expected timetable and deliverables, detailed goals of the project, and contact information for major stakeholders.

Also in the brief, designers usually get some insight into what the client thinks will make a successful project. This likely won't be spelled out; it may just be a throw-away line like "We want to make the new application fresh" embedded within a 50-page document filled with complicated business and technical goals. But if the designer meets all those goals but creates a conservative design that doesn't address the client's desire for "freshness," the client will be unhappy.

The brief should be only a starting point in discussions about the project. Indeed, the brief could raise as many questions as it solves. What exactly does making the application "fresh" mean? That's where stakeholder interviews come in. Stakeholders are clients who have a particular interest in, and influence on the outcome of, the project.

Stakeholder interviews (**Figure 2.1**) are usually one of the designer's first tasks on any project. The interviews are the client's chance to tell the designer why the client thinks that the project is needed. As stated earlier

Figure 2.1

Stakeholder interviews allow the client to explain the business goals of the project.

in this chapter, these reasons may be mistaken, and the designer should feel free to challenge them. The problem may not be what the client thinks it is.

Stakeholder interviews work best when they cast a wide net, so designers should take the time needed to conduct them well. The designer will want to interview not only those who are sponsoring the project (that is, putting up the money and resources), but also those in the organization who will be affected by the project. Often, people lower on the organization chart have deeper insights into the parameters of a project than those higher up. For example, consider a redesign of an application through which customers contact customer service. Although the project may be sponsored by the chief information officer and run by the director of customer service, the designer would be remiss if he or she didn't speak with the people who actually work with those contacts: the customer service representatives.

Business Goals

It's always the goal of an interaction designer to balance the goals of the business with the needs, abilities, and goals of the users. We'll spend considerable time thinking about users later, but stakeholder interviews are the time for the client to tell the designer (or for the designer to probe about) the business goals of the project. Business goals can be anything from hard numbers ("We need to sell 5 million ball bearings a day") to soft, company-brand goals ("We need a more elegant interface"). But again, the designer needs to be careful. Look for the *unstated* goals of the project. Sometimes, organizations want to use projects for different ends, such as to merge two departments or add staff, and will use the design project as a means to do so. Solutions that run contrary to these unstated goals may be greeted coldly.

By learning about the business goals of the project, the designer should also learn about what the organization will consider a successful project at the end ("We sold 10 million ball bearings today!")—that is, the project's *success metrics*. Success metrics let you take an objective look at a project's result to see what progress has been made toward its goal.

Evaluating success, of course, is much easier for projects with hard-numbers expectations than for those with softer goals. It's sometimes not easy to measure what businesses call return on investment (ROI) for interaction design. If an organization expects a design to meet an ROI goal, the designer needs to be sure some mechanism for measuring success is in place *before* the design work begins. Designers should have some sort of baseline criteria culled from the existing situation that they can then use to measure the new design against. For example, before beginning the redesign of a Web site registration process, the designer should get some quantitative data—numbers, in other words: "It takes six minutes to register; on an ease-of-use scale of 1 to 5, with 5 being excellent, users currently rate registration as a 2; according to server logs, half the people stop registering after the second page." With this baseline data in hand, at the end of the project, the designer can measure the new solution and compare the new data to the old and also to the goals of the project. If the designer has done the job well, the numbers will likely show it.

Constraints

Stakeholder interviews also help designers understand the *constraints* of the project. No project is without some boundaries that for business, technical, or time reasons cannot be crossed—at least not crossed easily. Constraints can be placed by a number of entities, such as marketing, accounting, management, IT, and of course, users. Sometimes constraints are as simple as the medium in which the project will be created ("We want a Web site" or "We want a new mobile device"). Sometimes constraints are a lot more complex ("We've already sold advertising for each Web page, so you need to design space for that" or "This robot can make only left turns right now and occasionally explodes"). Interaction designers need to capture and document constraints throughout the course of the project, in everything from stakeholder interview notes to wireframes (see Chapter 5). These constraints will often shape the design decisions that are made.

Designers can sometimes overcome constraints by coming up with a brilliant solution that can be implemented only by breaking a constraint, and then passionately arguing for it. For example, say a designer is working on a banking application. During research, users report that they absolutely need to see their account balances on every page to make good decisions. But one of the technical constraints is that the system cannot show balances on every page. What should the designer do? It's a choice between giving users what they need or living with constraints. I hope the designer would argue for breaking the constraint.

Gathering Information

Unless specifically told not to, designers should feel free to consult outside sources as part of the information-gathering process. Thanks to a little thing called the Internet, we now have access to information quickly and easily from many different sources. Designers should make good use of it. Very few projects are in an area that no one has thought about before. Even a cursory search of the Internet, and especially of e-mail list archives, discussion boards, and technical and academic journals, will likely turn up information about the project's subject area, whatever that may be.

As any doctoral candidate can attest, a person can spend a nearly infinite amount of time gathering information. It's important to focus this part of the process on gathering *germane* information that will eventually find its way into the solution. The goal is to gain general knowledge about the project's subject area (and perhaps related areas), and also deep knowledge about the particular problem that is being addressed. Interaction designers should not only ask the How and What questions, but also the Why questions. Why does this work this way? Why is it important to sell a million ball bearings a month? Why should this application be on a mobile phone? Why questions help designers avoid questions that don't provide much information, such as those that can be answered with a yes or no.

It's a good idea to spend only a fixed amount of time gathering information. Eventually, you need to stop defining the project and actually start designing it.

Four Approaches to Interaction Design

Once the designer has a problem (or, in designspeak, an opportunity) and has examined it from several angles to determine what lies at the core of the situation, the designer is ready to start finding a solution. There are four major approaches to finding solutions. All four have been used to create successful products, and it is typically up to designers to use the ones that work best for them. A few assertions apply to all these approaches:

▸   They can be used in many different situations to create vastly different products and services, from Web sites to consumer electronics to nondigital services.

▶ Most problematic situations can be improved by deploying at least one of these approaches to solving the problem.

▶ The best designers are those who can move between approaches, applying the best approach to the situation, and sometimes applying multiple approaches even within a single project.

▶ An individual designer will probably gravitate toward one of these approaches more than others. Some of these approaches simply may feel wrong. Designers generally work with the approaches they feel most comfortable employing. At different times, however, another approach may be the best way to solve a design problem, so it is important that interaction designers know all four approaches.

The four approaches are these:

▶ User-centered design (UCD)

▶ Activity-centered design

▶ Systems design

▶ Genius design

Table 2.1 provides a quick comparison of the four approaches.

TABLE 2.1   Four Approaches to Design

Approach	Overview	Users	Designer
User-Centered Design	Focuses on user needs and goals	Guide the design	Translates user needs and goals
Activity-Centered Design	Focuses on the tasks and activities that need to be accomplished	Perform the activities	Creates tools for actions
Systems Design	Focuses on the components of a system	Set the goals of the system	Makes sure all the parts of the system are in place
Genius Design	Relies on the skill and wisdom of designers used to make products	Source of validation	Is the source of inspiration

We'll look in detail at each of these approaches, starting with the one that is currently the most popular: user-centered design.

User-Centered Design

The philosophy behind user-centered design is simply this: users know best. The people who will be using a product or service know what their needs, goals, and preferences are, and it is up to the designer to find out those things and design for them. One shouldn't design a service for selling coffee without first talking to coffee drinkers. Designers, however well-meaning, aren't the users. Designers are involved simply to help users achieve their goals. Participation from users is sought (ideally) at every stage of the design process. Indeed, some practitioners of user-centered design view users as co-creators.

The concept of user-centered design has been around for a long time; its roots are in industrial design and ergonomics and in the belief that designers should try to fit products to people instead of the other way around. Industrial designer Henry Dreyfuss, who designed the iconic 500-series telephone for Bell Telephones, first popularized the method with his 1955 book *Designing for People*. But while industrial designers remembered this legacy, software engineers were blissfully unaware of it, and for decades they churned out software that made sense in terms of the way computers work, but not in terms of the way that people work. To be fair, this focus was not all the engineers' fault; with the limited processing speed and memory of computers for the first 40 years of their existence, it's sometimes astounding that engineers could make computers useful at all. The constraints of the system were huge. There was little concern for the user because it took so much effort and development time simply to get the computer to work correctly.

In the 1980s, designers and computer scientists working in the new field of human-computer interaction began questioning the practice of letting engineers design the interface for computer systems. With increased memory, processing speed, and color monitors, different types of interfaces were now possible, and a movement began to focus the design of computer software on users, not on computers. This movement became known as user-centered design (UCD).

Goals are really important in UCD; designers focus on what the user ultimately wants to accomplish. The designer then determines the tasks and means necessary to achieve those goals, but always with the users' needs and preferences in mind.

In the best (or at least most thorough) UCD approach, designers involve users in every stage of the project. Designers consult users at the beginning of the project to see if the proposed project will even address the users' needs. Designers conduct extensive research (see Chapter 4) up front to determine what the users' goals are in the current situation. Then, as designers develop models related to the project (see Chapter 5), they consult users about them. Designers (often alongside usability professionals) test prototypes with users as well.

Simply put, throughout the project, user data is the determining factor in making design decisions. When a question arises as to how something should be done, the users' wants and needs determine the response. For example, if during user research for an e-commerce Web site, users say they want the shopping cart in the upper-right corner of the page, when the shopping cart is ultimately positioned on the page, that's likely where the shopping cart will be.

The real targets of UCD—user goals—are notoriously slippery and often hard to define, especially long-term goals. Or else they are so vague that it is nearly impossible to design for them. Let's say a designer is creating an application to help college students manage their schedules. What's the goal there? To help students do better in school? But why? So they can graduate? What's the goal there? To get a good job? To become educated? User goals can quickly become like Russian dolls, with goals nestled inside goals.

That being said, what UCD is best at is getting designers to move away from their own preferences and instead to focus on the needs and goals of the users, and this result should not be undervalued. Designers, like everyone else, carry around their own experiences and prejudices, and those can conflict with what users require in a product or service. A UCD approach removes designers from that trap. One design dictum is "You are not the user."

UCD doesn't always work, however. Relying on users for all design insights can sometimes result in a product or service that is too narrowly focused. Designers may, for instance, be basing their work on the wrong set or type of users. For products that will be used by millions of people, UCD may be impractical. UCD is a valuable approach, but it is only one approach to design.

Activity-Centered Design

Activity-centered design doesn't focus on the goals and preferences of users, but instead on activities. Activities can be loosely defined as a cluster of actions and decisions that are done for a purpose. Activities can be brief and simple (making a sandwich) or time consuming and involved (learning a foreign language). Activities can take moments or years. You can do them alone or with others, as is the case, for example, when you sing a song. Some activities, such as withdrawing money from an ATM, have a set ending—in this case, getting the money. Others, such as listening to music, have no fixed ending. The activity simply stops when the actor (or some outside force) decides it is over.

Many products we use today were designed using activity-centered design, especially functional tools like appliances and cars. Activity-centered design allows designers to tightly focus on the work at hand and create support for the activity itself instead of more distant goals (**Figure 2.2**). Thus, it's well-suited for complicated actions.

The *purpose* of an activity is not necessarily a *goal*. Purposes are generally more focused and tangible than goals. Consider the activity of raking leaves, for example. The gardener may have a goal (to have a tidy yard), but the purpose of using a rake is simple: to collect leaves.

Of course, sometimes goals and purposes can be the same or similar. For example, in the activity of making tea, the goal and the purpose are pretty much the same: to drink tea. Few people have as a goal to become a master tea brewer.

Activities are made up of actions and decisions. Designers call these *tasks*. Tasks can be as discrete as pushing a button or as complicated as performing all the steps necessary to launch a nuclear missile. The purpose of tasks is to engage in (and possibly complete) an activity. Each task is a moment in the life of the activity.

Figure 2.2

A cello is a product designed for one specific activity: making music.

Consider the simple activity of buying a new game for a game console. Here are the tasks:

▶ Decide to buy a new game.

▶ Decide what game to buy.

▶ Decide where to buy it.

▶ Get directions to store if necessary.

▶ Go to store.

▶ Enter store.

▶ Find game in store.

▶ Buy game.

▶ Leave store.

▶ Go home.

As this example shows, the difference between a task and an activity can be fairly minor. Some tasks have enough parts to them to be considered sub-activities unto themselves. For example, in making a phone call, one of the tasks is finding the right number to dial. There are quite a few ways to find a phone number: call a service for assistance, look up the number in a phone book, recall the number from memory, and so on. Each of these solutions to the task of finding a number is itself a task. So is finding a phone number a task or an activity? For designers, the difference is usually academic.

Like user-centered design, activity-centered design relies on research as the basis for its insights, albeit not as heavily. Designers observe and interview users for insights about their behavior more than about their goals. Designers catalog users' activities and tasks, perhaps add some missing tasks, and then design solutions to help users accomplish the task, not achieve a goal per se.

Ultimately, activity-centered design allows designers to focus narrowly on the tasks at hand and design products and services that support those tasks. The task "submit form" will probably require a button. The task "turn device on" will probably require a switch. And so on. The activity, not the people doing the activity, guides the design.

Activity-centered design can be ethically tricky. Some tasks require skill—sometimes great skill—and designers shouldn't ignore this in design-ing alternatives. Removing or automating people's valuable skills can be morally troubling. It may take weeks to learn a call-center's software, for instance. But then again, perhaps the reason the software takes weeks to learn is because it's poorly designed. Designers should be especially careful in choosing the tasks they automate; it is very easy to de-skill users, to remove tasks that may be tedious or difficult to learn, but are also pleasurable to perform. Imagine being asked to design a piano that was easier to learn and play! We'll talk more about ethics and design in the epilogue, "Designing for Good."

Another danger in activity-centered design is that by fixating on tasks, designers won't look for solutions for the problem as a whole. They won't see the forest for the trees. There's an old design adage: You'll get a different result if you tell people to design a vase than if you tell them to design something to hold flowers. By focusing on small tasks, designers can find themselves designing vase after vase and never a hanging garden.

Systems Design

Systems design is a very analytical way of approaching design problems; it uses an established arrangement of components to create design solutions. Whereas in user-centered design, the user is at the center of the design process, here a system—a set of entities that act upon each other—is. A system isn't necessarily a computer, although it can be. Systems can also consist of people, devices, machines, and objects. Systems can range from the simple (the heating system in your house) to the enormously complex (whole governments).

Systems design is a structured, rigorous design methodology that is excellent for tackling complex problems and that offers a holistic approach to designing. Systems design doesn't discount user goals and needs—they can be used to set the goal of the system. But in this approach, users are deemphasized in favor of *context*. Designers using systems design focus on the whole context of use, not just individual objects or devices. Systems design can be thought of as a rigorous look at the broad context in which a product or service will be used.

Systems design outlines the components that systems should have: a goal, a sensor, a comparator, and an actuator. The job of the designer, then, becomes designing those components. In this way, systems design eliminates the guesswork and fuzziness of the other approaches and provides a clear roadmap for designers to follow.

Let's use the classic example of a heating system to illustrate the main parts of any system (**Figure 2.3**).

Figure 2.3

A system, based on
a diagram by Hugh
Dubberly and Paul
Pangaro, 2003.

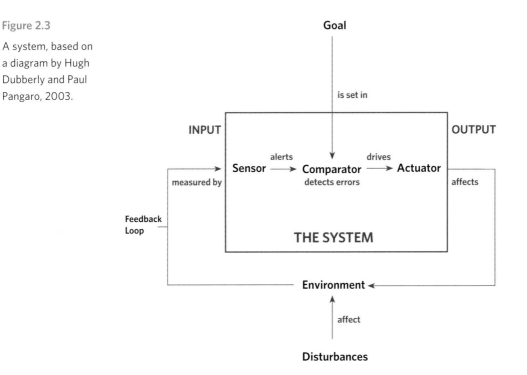

▷ **Goal.** This is not the users' goal, but rather the goal of the system as a whole, which can be drawn from user goals. The goal states the ideal relationship between the system and the environment it lives in. In a heating system, an example of a goal is keeping your house at 72 degrees Fahrenheit.

▷ **Environment.** Where does the system "live"? Is it digital or analog or both? The environment in the heating system example is the house itself.

▷ **Sensors.** How does the system detect changes in the environment? A heating system has a thermostat with a thermometer (**Figure 2.4**) to detect temperature changes.

▶ **Disturbances.** Changes are called disturbances; these are elements in the environment that change the environment in both expected and unexpected ways. In the heating system example, a disturbance is a drop in temperature. More on disturbances in a moment.

▶ **Comparator.** The comparator embodies the goal within the system. It compares the current state (the environment) to the desired state (the goal). Any difference between the two is seen by the system as an error, which the system seeks to correct. In the heating system example, the comparator can be a tiny computer or a mercury switch that compares what the sensor tells it about the environment (for example, "72 degrees…72 degrees…72 degrees…71 degrees…71 degrees") to the goal ("Keep the house at 72 degrees").

Figure 2.4

A thermostat contains the sensor, comparator, actuator, and controls of a heating system.

▶ **Actuator.** If the sensor detects a disturbance, the comparator says, ah, something is different (an "error"), and it sends a command to the actuator (in this case, the boiler). Actuators are a means of making changes (output) to the environment. In this case, the actuator makes heat.

▶ **Feedback.** With output comes feedback. Feedback is a message about whether or not a goal was achieved or maintained—whether or not an error was detected. In the heating system example, feedback would report either that the house is still at 71 degrees or that it is now at 72 degrees and the heater can be turned off.

▶ **Controls.** Controls are means of manually manipulating the parts of the system (except the environment). In this example, you use a control to set the temperature you want the house to be. Another control might trigger the actuator and turn the heat on.

There are two types of disturbances to the environment that may affect our heating system. The first consists of expected disturbances, such as the periodic drops in temperature. The second type consists of unexpected disturbances—things that fall outside of the expected range of input. These types of disturbances typically cause the system to crash or behave in odd ways. In our heating example, such an event might be a sudden 100-degree drop in temperature.

To make most unexpected disturbances expected (and thus make the system more stable), systems need what's called *requisite variety*. The system needs an assortment of responses to deal with a range of situations. These responses can be anything from error messages ("You are being sent 1 million e-mail messages!"), to workarounds ("You are being sent 1 million e-mail messages. Should I delete them or deliver them in chunks of 10,000?"), to mechanisms to prevent the system from failing (deleting all incoming e-mails over a certain number). Systems without requisite variety crash often, which may be fine for a prototype, but not so great for, say, an air-traffic control system.

Feedback is output from the system that reports that something has just happened: input was received from the environment, the comparator was changed, and so on. You get feedback from your computer almost every time you press a key. We'll discuss feedback in more detail in Chapter 3, but we'll simply note here that systems without feedback either will not work or will be bewildering.

Systems design isn't only about digital products, of course. Most services (see Chapter 8), for example, are systems consisting of digital and analog components. Your local coffee shop is filled with sensors, comparators, and actuators, only you probably know them as the shop employees. However, the objections and distaste many designers have about systems design spring from examples just such as these. Many designers feel that systems design is dehumanizing, turning people into robotic components in a very synthetic arrangement. And indeed, systems design is a very logical, analytical approach to interaction design. Emotions, passion, and whim have very little place in this sort of design, except as disturbances in the environment that need to be countered. Someone screaming angrily in the coffee shop is a major disturbance!

Systems design's greatest strength, however, is that it is useful for seeing the big picture—for providing a holistic view of a project. No product or service exists in a vacuum, after all, and systems design forces designers to take into account the environment that the product or service inhabits. By focusing on the broad context of use and the interplay of the components, designers gain a better understanding of the circumstances surrounding a product or service.

Hugh Dubberly on Systems Design

Hugh Dubberly is founder and principal at Dubberly Design Office (DDO), an interaction design consultancy in San Francisco. Before forming DDO, he served as vice president for design at AOL/Netscape and as creative director at Apple Computer, Inc. He has also taught at San Jose State University and Stanford University.

What is systems design?

Systems design is simply the design of systems. It implies a systematic and rigorous approach to design—an approach demanded by the scale and complexity of many systems problems.

Where did systems design come from?

Systems design first appeared shortly before World War II as engineers grappled with complex communications and control problems. They formalized their work in the new disciplines of information theory, operations research, and cybernetics. In the 1960s, members of the design methods movement (especially Horst Rittel and others at Ulm and Berkeley) transferred this knowledge to the design world. Systems design continues to flourish at schools interested in design planning and within the world of computer science. Among its most important legacies is a research field known as design rationale, which concerns systems for making and documenting design decisions.

What can designers learn from systems design?

Today, ideas from design methods and systems design may be more relevant to designers than ever before—as more and more designers collaborate on designing software and complex information spaces. Frameworks suggested by systems design are especially useful in modeling interaction and conversation. They are also useful in modeling the design process itself.

Hugh Dubberly on Systems Design Continued

What is the most important thing to be aware of in systems design?

A systems approach to design asks:

▶   For this situation, what is the system?

▶   What is the environment?

▶   What goal does the system have in relation to its environment?

▶   What is the feedback loop by which the system corrects its actions?

▶   How does the system measure whether it has achieved its goal?

▶   Who defines the system, environment, goal, and so on—and monitors it?

▶   What resources does the system have for maintaining the relationship it desires?

▶   Are the resources sufficient to meet the system's purpose?

Is systems design incompatible with user-centered design?

A systems approach to design is entirely compatible with a user-centered approach. Indeed, the core of both approaches is understanding user goals. A systems approach looks at users in relation to a context and in terms of their interaction with devices, with each other, and with themselves.

What is the relationship between systems design and cybernetics?

Cybernetics (the science of feedback) provides an approach to systems and a set of frameworks and tools. Among the most important ideas for designers:

▶   Definition of a system depends on point of view (subjectivity).

▶   We are responsible for our actions (ethical stance).

▶   All interaction is a form of conversation.

▶   All conversation involves goals, understandings, and agreements.

Are there times when systems design isn't appropriate?

A systems approach to design is most appropriate for projects involving large systems or systems of systems. Such projects typically involve many people, from many disciplines, working together over an extended period of time. They need tools to cope with their project's complexity: to define goals, facilitate communications, and manage processes. Solo designers working on small projects may find the same tools a bit cumbersome for their needs.

Genius Design

The fourth major design approach is something I call genius design. Genius design relies almost solely on the wisdom and experience of the designer to make design decisions. Designers use their best judgment as to what users want and then design the product based on that judgment. User involvement, if it occurs at all, comes at the end of the process, when users test what the designers have made to make sure it really works as the designer has predicted.

Compared to the rigor of the other three approaches, genius design seems almost cavalier. Yet this is how most interaction design is done today, either by choice—Apple, supposedly for security reasons, does no user research or testing at all—or by necessity. Many designers work in organizations that don't provide funding or time for research, so the designers are left to their own devices.

This is not to say that designers who practice genius design don't consider users—they do. It's simply that the designers either don't have the resources or the inclination to involve users in the design process. Designers use their personal knowledge (and frequently the knowledge of the organization they're working for and research from others) to determine users' wants, needs, and expectations.

Genius design can create some impressive designs, such as Apple's iPod (**Figure 2.5**). It can also create some impressive failures, such as Apple's first handheld device, the Newton. Aside from market forces (not an inconsiderable factor), the success of genius-designed products rests heavily on the skill of the designer. Thus, genius design is probably best practiced by experienced designers, who have encountered many different types of problems and can draw upon solutions from many past projects. It probably also works best when the designer is one of the potential

Figure 2.5

Apple's iPod was created using genius design by designers such as Jonathan Ive.

users, although this status can be a serious trap as well. The designers who created the Windows 95 operating system probably considered themselves the users, but while they understood how the OS worked perfectly well, ordinary users suffered. Because of their intimate understanding of how the product or service they designed was created and their inside knowledge of the decisions behind it, the designers will know much more about the functionality of the product or service than will most end users.

Unfortunately, while genius design is best practiced by experienced designers, it's often attempted by inexperienced designers. Many designers use this approach because it is, frankly, easier than the other three. It requires a lot less effort to noodle on a whiteboard than it does to research users or artfully assemble the components of a system. And while I am loathe to tell anyone not to trust their instincts, designers should practice genius design with care, for instincts can be dead wrong.

Genius design has many strengths, however, especially for an experienced designer. It's a fast and personal way to work, and the final design, perhaps more than with the other approaches, reflects the designer's own sensibilities. It is also the most flexible approach, allowing designers to focus their efforts where they see fit. By following their own muses, designers may be able to think more broadly and innovate more freely.

Summary

Most designers feel more comfortable with one design approach than others, although most designers mix approaches as they work. A designer's temperament, personal philosophy, and view of work and of a project's users will help determine which approach the designer prefers. But the best designers are those who can move between different approaches as the situation warrants, so it's good to know them all.

3

Interaction Design Basics

No matter what approach an interaction designer uses, the basic materials involved in solutions, such as motion, space, and time, remain the same. Likewise, the principles and ideas that guide and inform the design process also are the same: the "laws" such as Fitts' and Hick's, the Poka-Yoke Principle, feedback and feedforward, and direct and indirect manipulation.

We'll start with the building blocks of interaction design: the basic set of resources that interaction designers have to manipulate.

The Elements of Interaction Design

Other design disciplines use raw materials. Communication designers use basic visual elements such as the line. Industrial designers work with simple 3D shapes such as the cube, the sphere, and the cylinder. For interaction designers, who create products and services that can be digital (software) or analog (a karaoke machine) or both (a mobile phone), the design elements are more conceptual. And yet they offer a powerful set of components for interaction designers to bring to bear on their projects.

Motion

In much the same way that inert gases don't mingle with other gases, objects that don't move don't interact (**Figure 3.1**). An interaction, as noted in Chapter 1, is some sort of communication, and communication is about movement: our vocal cords vibrating as we speak, our hands and arms writing or typing as we send e-mail or instant messages, sound and data moving between two entities.

We communicate in many ways and through many different products, from mobile phones to e-mail. Those products and the people who use them generate *behavior*, and interaction designers are very concerned with behavior: the way that products behave in response to the way that people behave. And all behavior is, in fact, motion: motion colored by attitude, culture, personality, and context. There's wide variation even in such universal and seemingly simple behaviors such as walking (that's why, for instance, there's a need for both high-impact walking shoes and walkers for the elderly), and the designs we create have to understand and account for those variations. Even a simple motion like pressing a key on a keyboard can be difficult if you are elderly or infirm.

Figure 3.1

Motion. Without
motion, there can be
no interaction.

Motion is often a trigger for action, as when your finger clicks the button on your mouse. The triggered action (or at least the feedback for that action) is often about motion as well. You click a Web site link, and the page changes. You press a key, and an e-mail window closes. There is motion on your screen.

Without motion, there can be no interaction.

Space

Movement, even on a subatomic level, happens in some sort of space, even if the boundary of that space (as with, say, the Internet) is unclear. Interaction designers work in both 2D and 3D space, whether that space is a digital screen or the analog, physical space we all inhabit (**Figure 3.2**).

Most often, interaction design involves a combination of physical and digital spaces. You make a gesture in physical, analog space—for instance, turning a knob on your stereo—and you see the results on its digital display screen. The reverse can, of course, be true as well. You can stream music from your computer through your stereo and into physical space.

Figure 3.2

Space. All interactions take place in a space. This Italian piazza in Ferrara was designed for interaction.

Most interaction designers underutilize 3D space on screens. The physical flatness of our monitors and display screens causes us to ignore what the Renaissance painters discovered so long ago: perspective. Objects, even in a 2D space, can appear to move backward and forward in 3D space. Perspective creates, alongside X (height) and Y (width), a Z (depth) axis on which to work. Web sites are notably bad in their use of Z space.

Starbucks cafes typically make excellent use of physical space, with the ordering area separated from the fulfillment area where customers receive their beverages, and those areas separated from the area where people can customize (add milk and sugar and other condiments to) their drinks. Compare that to the typical crush around a single counter of a fast food restaurant.

Space provides a context for motion. Is the action taking place in a quiet office in front of a computer screen or in a crowded, noisy airport in front of a kiosk?

All interactions take place in a space.

Time

All interactions take place over time. Sometimes an interaction can occur instantaneously, as with a mouse click. Sometimes it can involve very long durations (**Figure 3.3**). You can still find online Usenet messages (Usenet is a sort of bulletin board system) from decades ago.

Movement through space takes time to accomplish. As every gamer will attest, it takes time to press buttons (around 8 milliseconds at the fastest). Even with broadband speeds, it takes time for packets of data to travel from distant servers through the physical wires and perhaps through the air via wireless signal to your computer.

Interaction designers need an awareness of time. Some tasks are complicated and take a long time to complete—for instance, searching for and buying a product. Many e-commerce Web sites require you to log in before making a purchase, and that login session will be active for a set time. Imagine if Amazon or other e-commerce sites timed out every few minutes and required you to log in repeatedly while shopping—it's unlikely you'd buy much from them. Some travel and concert-ticket Web sites make users race against the clock to enter their credit card information before their selected seats are lost.

Digital time is definitely not human time. Digital time is measured in milliseconds, a single one of which is considerably shorter than the blink of an eye. Changes made by the computer can be so nearly instantaneous that programmers need to program in delays so that humans can detect them.

You can feel the impact of milliseconds, however. Extra milliseconds added to every keystroke or mouse-click would probably make you think

Figure 3.3

Time. All interactions take place over time. Sometimes this time can be very brief, and sometimes it can be very long indeed.

your computer is slow because of the tiny delays. Several hundred milliseconds would cause frustration and anger, and a single-second delay each time you pressed a key would probably make your computer unusable.

Time creates rhythm. How fast a menu pops up on the screen or how long it takes to complete an action such as renewing your driver's license controls the rhythm of the interaction. Games are often alert to rhythm: how many aliens come at you at any given moment or how long it takes to complete a level. Rhythm is also an important component of animation: how quickly does a folder open or close on the desktop, how slowly does a drop-down menu slide open. Interaction designers control this rhythm.

Battery life (the duration of which is slowly getting better) is another element of time of which designers need to be cognizant. Some features, such as a backlight, drain more battery power than others and thus decrease the amount of time a device works. A mobile phone that worked for only 10 minutes when unplugged from a power outlet wouldn't be of much use.

Interactions happen over time.

Appearance

How something looks gives us cues as to how it behaves and how we should interact with it (**Figure 3.4**). The size, shape, and even weight of mobile devices let us know that they should be carried with us. The sleek black or silver look of digital video recorders like TiVo devices tells us that they are pieces of electronic equipment and belong alongside stereos and televisions.

Appearance is one major source (texture is the other) of what cognitive psychologist James Gibson, in 1966, called *affordances*. Gibson explored the concept more fully in his 1979 book *The Ecological Approach to Visual Perception,* but it wasn't until Don Norman's seminal book *The Psychology of Everyday Things,* in 1988, that the term spread into design. An affordance is a property, or multiple properties, of an object that provides some indication of how to interact with that object or with a feature on that object. A chair has an affordance of sitting because of its shape. A button has an affordance of pushing because of its shape and the way it moves (or seemingly moves). The empty space in a cup is an affordance that tells us we could fill the cup with liquid.

Affordances (or, technically, *perceived* affordances) are contextual and cultural. You know you can push a button because you've pushed one before. On the other hand, a person who has never seen chopsticks may be puzzled about what to do with them.

Figure 3.4

Appearance. The design of this gate latch provides affordances indicating how it should be used.

Except to the visually impaired (for whom texture often substitutes), appearance also conveys emotional content. Is this product whimsical or serious? Practical or playful? Appearance can also convey other attributes that may be meaningful: Is the object expensive or cheap? Complicated or simple? Daunting or approachable? Single use or enduring? Structured or casual?

Appearance has many variables for designers to alter:

- Proportion
- Structure
- Size
- Shape
- Weight
- Color (hue, value, saturation)

All of these characteristics (and more) add up to appearance, and nearly every design has some sort of appearance, even if that appearance is a simple command line.

Texture

While texture can also be part of the appearance, how an object *feels* in the hand can convey the same sort of information as appearance (**Figure 3.5**). Texture, too, can convey affordances. The sensation of an object can provide clues as to how it is to be used as well as when and where. Is it solid or flimsy? Is it fragile or durable? Do the knobs spin or push or do both?

Figure 3.5

Texture. How something feels in the hand can also provide affordances indicating how it could be used, as in the case of these cane lobster traps.

Texture can convey emotion as well. A fuzzy, plush object conveys a different meaning than a hard, metallic one.

Designers can also work with texture variables such as vibration and heat to signify actions. A mobile phone can vibrate when a new message arrives, and one could imagine it growing colder the longer it's been since a voice-mail message arrived.

Sound

Sound (**Figure 3.6**) is a small part of most interaction designs, but it can be an important part, especially for alerts and ambient devices (see Chapter 7). Sound possesses many variables that can convey information as well. You wouldn't want a loud screech to come out of your computer every time you received e-mail, and a soft whisper wouldn't cause traffic to move aside for an ambulance.

Figure 3.6

Sound. Sound can be manipulated as a tool of interaction design through devices such as this mixing board.

Sounds are made up of three main components, all of which can be adjusted by a designer:

▶ **Pitch.** How high in range a sound is. Is it high pitched like a bird's song or deep like thunder?

▶ **Volume.** How loud a sound is.

▶ **Timbre or tone quality.** What type of sound it is. Sounds played at the same volume and pitch can seem very different. Think of a middle C played on a trumpet and one played on a piano.

Sound is underutilized (some would say rightfully so) in interaction design, but even a little bit of sound can make a major difference in a product. Steve Jobs insisted that the iPod's wheel make an audible click that could be heard without headphones.

All of these elements of interaction design comprise any interaction designer's toolkit, and while interaction designers may not consciously manipulate them, they are the building blocks of interaction design. Now let's look at some principles that should guide the way that interaction designers assemble these elements into a product or service.

The Laws of Interaction Design

Interaction design, being a new field, doesn't have very many hard and fast rules, or "laws," to speak of. In a sense, interaction designers are still figuring out many of the basic principles of the work they do. However, there are a handful of laws that interaction designers have used successfully. Except for Moore's Law, which designers need only understand, not put into practice, these laws should guide the work, not dictate it.

Moore's Law

In 1965, Gordon Moore, a co-founder of microchip maker Intel, predicted that every two years, the number of transistors on integrated circuits (a rough measure of computer processing power) will double.

Amazingly, this is exactly what has occurred and is still occurring, with staggering results. There is more processing power in a modern laptop than in all of NASA's Mission Control Center when the space agency sent a man to the moon in 1969. The fulfillment of Moore's Law is the underpinning for everything from color monitors to video teleconferencing to the ability to run multiple programs at once. Designers can conceive of devices that are faster, smaller, and more powerful than could feasibly have been considered even a decade ago, much less in 1965 when Moore made his prediction. And in two more years, our devices will be faster, smaller, and more powerful still.

Fitts' Law

Published in 1954 by psychologist Paul Fitts, Fitts' (pronounced "fitzez") Law simply states that the time it takes to move from a starting position to a final target is determined by two factors: the distance to the target and the size of the target. Fitts' Law models the act of pointing, both with a finger and with a device like a mouse. The larger the target, the faster it can be pointed to. Likewise, the closer the target, the faster it can be pointed to.

Fitts' Law has three main implications for interaction designers. Since the size of the target matters, clickable objects like buttons need to be reasonable sizes. As anyone who has tried to click a tiny icon will attest, the smaller the object, the harder it is to manipulate. Second, the edges and corners of screens are excellent places to position things like menu bars and buttons. Edges and corners are huge targets because they basically have infinite height or width. You can't overshoot them with the mouse; your mouse will stop on the edge of the screen no matter how far you move it, and thus will land on top of the button or menu. The third major implication of Fitts' Law is that pop-up menus that appear next to the object that a person is working on (such as a menu that appears next to an object when the user right-clicks the mouse) can usually be opened more quickly than can pull-down menus at the top of the screen, which require travel to other parts of the screen.

Hick's Law

Hick's Law, or the Hick-Hyman Law, says that the time it takes for users to make decisions is determined by the number of possible choices they have. People don't consider a group of possible choices one by one. Instead, they subdivide the choices into categories, eliminating about half of the remaining choices with each step in the decision. Thus, Hick's Law claims that a user will more quickly make choices from one menu of 10 items than from two menus of 5 items each.

A controversial implication of this law is that it is better for products to give users many choices simultaneously instead of organizing the choices into hierarchical groups, as in drop-down menus. If followed to an extreme, this approach could create some truly frightening designs. Imagine if a content-rich site like Yahoo or Amazon presented all of its links on the home page, or if your mobile phone displayed all of its features on its main screen.

Hick's Law also states that the time it takes to make a decision is affected by two factors: familiarity with the choices, such as from repeated use, and the format of the choices—are they sounds or words, videos or buttons?

The Magical Number Seven

Hick's Law seems to run counter to George Miller's Magical Number Seven rule. In 1956, Miller, a Princeton University psychology professor, determined that the human mind is best able to remember information in chunks of seven items, "plus or minus two." After five to nine pieces of information (for instance, navigation labels or a list of features or a set of numbers), the human mind starts making errors. It seems that we have difficulty keeping more than that amount of information in our short-term memory at any given time.

Some designers have taken the Magical Number Seven rule to an extreme, making sure that there are never any more than seven items on a screen at any given time. This is a bit excessive, because Miller was specifically talking about bits of information that humans have to remember or visualize in short-term memory. When those bits of information are displayed on a screen, users don't have to keep them in their short-term memory; they can always refer to them.

But designers should take care not to design a product that causes cognitive overload by ignoring the Magical Number Seven rule. For example, designers should never create a device that forces users to remember unfamiliar items across screens or pages. Imagine if you had to type a new phone number on three separate screens of your mobile phone. You'd scramble to do so (if you could!) before the number faded from your short-term memory.

Tesler's Law of the Conservation of Complexity

Larry Tesler, one of the pioneers of interaction design (see the interview with him later in this chapter), coined Tesler's Law of the Conservation of Complexity, which states that some complexity is inherent to every process. There is a point beyond which you can't simplify a process any further; you can only move the inherent complexity from one place to another.

For example, for an e-mail message, two elements are required: your e-mail address and the address of the person to whom you are sending the mail. If either of these items is missing, the e-mail can't be sent, and your e-mail client will tell you so. It's a necessary complexity. But some of that burden has likely been shifted to your e-mail client. You don't typically have to enter your e-mail address every time you send e-mail; the e-mail program handles that task for you. Likewise, the e-mail client probably also helps you by remembering e-mail addresses to which you've sent mail in the past, so that you don't have to remember them and type them in fully each time. The complexity isn't gone, though—instead, some of it has been shifted to the software.

Interaction designers need to be aware of Tesler's Law for two reasons. First, designers need to acknowledge that all processes have elements that cannot be made simpler, no matter how much we tinker with them. As The Who told us in their 1966 song "Substitute," the simple things you see are all complicated. Second, designers need to look for reasonable places to move this complexity into the products they make. It doesn't make sense for users to type their e-mail addresses in every e-mail they send when software can handle this task. The burden of complexity needs to be shared as much as possible by the products interaction designers make.

Larry Tesler on the Laws of Interaction Design

Larry Tesler's resume reads like the history of interaction design. He's worked at Xerox PARC, Apple, and Amazon and is now at Yahoo as vice president of the User Experience and Design group. While at Xerox PARC, he helped develop some of the language of interaction design, including pop-up menus and cut-and-paste editing. His law of the Conservation of Complexity (discussed in this chapter) is known to programmers and designers alike.

You've worked at some of the seminal places for interaction design: Xerox PARC, Apple, Amazon, and now Yahoo. What do they all have in common?

All of them place a high value on both advanced technology and customer delight.

Are there any unbreakable "laws" in interaction design?

Just one. Design for the users.

Larry Tesler on the Laws of Interaction Design *Continued*

How did you come up with Tesler's Law of the Conservation of Complexity?

In the early days of our field, when I worked at Xerox PARC, the idea of user interface consistency was new and controversial. Many of us realized that consistency would benefit not only users, but also developers, because standards could be encapsulated in shared software libraries. We made an economic argument: If we establish standards and encourage consistency, we can reduce time to market and code size.

In 1983–1985, when I was developing the Mac app object-oriented framework at Apple, I advocated a three-layer code model. In addition to the Macintosh Toolbox—a shared software library—and the application itself, I made the case for an intermediate layer that implemented what I called a generic application. A generic application was a real interactive program—with windows, menus, and commands—that did nothing at all, but did it in a standard way. You could create, open, save, and print documents, but the documents lacked form and were empty of content. You built your actual application by modifying the generic application in an object-oriented way.

To sell the idea to Apple management and independent software vendors, I came up with the Law of Conservation of Complexity. I postulated that every application must have an inherent amount of irreducible complexity. The only question is who will have to deal with it.

Because computers back then were small, slow, and expensive, programs were designed to be compact, not easy to use. The user had to deal with complexity because the programmer couldn't. But commercial software is written once and used millions of times. If a million users each waste a minute a day dealing with complexity that an engineer could have eliminated in a week by making the software a little more complex, you are penalizing the user to make the engineer's job easier.

Whose time is more important to the success of your business? For mass-market software, unless you have a sustainable monopoly position, the customer's time has to be more important to you than your own.

What personal qualities do you think make a good interaction designer?

Enough confidence to believe you can solve any design problem and enough humility to understand that most of your initial ideas are probably bad. Enough humility to listen to ideas from other people that may be better than your own and enough confidence to understand that going with other people's ideas does not diminish your value as a designer.

True concern for the comfort and happiness of other people, including your users and your teammates. If you're not teammate friendly, your products won't be user friendly. That does not mean you should cave in under pressure on an important issue when you have data that supports your opinion. But it does mean you should judge success by the success of the product and the team, not just by the success of your own narrow contribution.

There are a lot of other desirable personal qualities for a designer, such as attention to detail, objectivity, appreciation of humor, appreciation of esthetics, and appreciation of data about users and usage.

The Poka-Yoke Principle

Legendary Japanese industrial engineer and quality guru Shigeo Shingo created the Poka-Yoke Principle in 1961 while working for Toyota. Poka-yoke roughly translates in English to mistake proofing: avoiding (*yokeru*) inadvertent errors (*poka*). Designers use poka-yoke when they put constraints on products to prevent errors, forcing users to adjust their behavior and correctly execute an operation.

Simple examples of the application of poka-yoke are the cords (USB, FireWire, power, and others) that fit into electronic devices only in a particular way and in a particular place, and thus prevent someone from, say, plugging the power cord into the hole where the headphones go (**Figure 3.7**). In this way, poka-yoke ensures that proper conditions exist *before* a process begins, preventing problems from occurring in the first place. Poka-yoke can be implemented in lots of forms: by signs (Do not touch the third rail!), procedures (Step 1: Unplug toaster), humans (police directing traffic around an accident), or any other entity that prevents incorrect execution of a process step. Where prevention is not possible, poka-yoke mandates that problems be stopped as early as possible in the process. Interaction designers should look for opportunities to use the Poka-Yoke Principle.

Figure 3.7

An illustration of the Poka-Yoke Principle. The USB cord will fit into only a particular slot on this laptop computer.

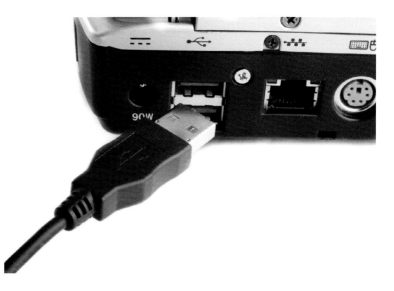

Direct and Indirect Manipulation

Digital objects can be manipulated in two ways: directly and indirectly. Although technically digital objects can be manipulated only indirectly (you can't touch something that's made of bits and bytes, after all), direct and indirect manipulation represent two ways of thinking about how to work with digital objects.

Direct manipulation is a term coined by University of Maryland professor Ben Shneiderman in the early 1980s. It refers to the process in which, by selecting a digital object with a finger or with a mouse or some other extension of the hand (which is really direct manipulation in and of itself), we can then do something to the object: move it, turn it, drag it to the trash, change its color, and so on. We can mimic an action that we might perform on a similar object in the physical world. For example, we can scale an object by dragging a corner of it as though we were stretching it. Direct manipulation, because it more closely maps to our physical experiences, is supposedly more easily learned and used, especially for manipulating 3D objects in digital space.

In indirect manipulation, we use a command or menu or other means that isn't directly a part of the digital object to alter that object. Choosing the Select All command in the application interface and pressing the Delete key on the keyboard are examples of indirect manipulation. In the past, especially during the years before the Macintosh popularized the GUI, nearly all computer commands were indirect.

Interaction designers need to decide how digital objects in their products can be manipulated: directly, indirectly, or (more and more frequently) in both ways.

Feedback and Feedforward

Feedback, as it is commonly used, is some indication that something has happened. Feedback should occur like crooked voting does: early and often. Every action by a person who engages with the product or service, no matter how slightly, should be accompanied by some acknowledgment of the action: Moving the mouse should move the cursor. Pressing a key on your mobile phone should display a number.

Proceeding otherwise is to court errors, some of them potentially serious. Frequently, if there is no immediate or obvious feedback, users will repeat the action they just did—for instance, pushing a button twice. Needless to say, this can cause problems, such as accidentally buying an item twice or transferring money multiple times. If the button is connected to dangerous machinery, it could result in injury or death. People need feedback.

We know that feedback is essential; designing the *appropriate* feedback is the designer's task. The designer has to determine how quickly the product or service will respond and in what manner. Should the response be something simple such as the appearance of a letter on a screen (the feedback in word processing for pressing a key), or should it be a complex indicator such as a pattern of blinking LED lights on a device that monitors your stock portfolio?

Related to feedback (and also to affordances) is what designer Tom Djajadiningrat calls *feedforward*: knowing what will happen *before* you perform an action. Feedforward can be a straightforward message ("Pushing this button will submit your order") or simple cues such as hypertext links with descriptive names instead of "Here."

Feedforward allows users to perform an action with confidence because it gives them an idea of what will happen next. Feedforward is harder to design into products and services than feedback, but designers should keep an eye out for opportunities to use it.

Characteristics of Good Interaction Design

In almost all designs, no matter for what, digital or analog, interaction designers should strive to reflect the following set of adjectives. Certainly in some circumstances, some of these characteristics may not be appropriate—you may not want a mission control panel to be playful, for example—but in general, if a product or service can be described with these adjectives, it is likely an example of good interaction design.

Trustworthy

Before we'll use a tool, we have to trust that it can do the job. You wouldn't pick up a rusty hammer with a loose handle to drive in nails—you wouldn't trust it to not smash your thumb. The same holds true for digital products and for services. Given a choice, you wouldn't eat in a filthy restaurant or use a mobile phone that only occasionally rang when someone called.

Humans likely make decisions about the trustworthiness of a product or service within seconds of engaging with it. Indeed, recent research has suggested that humans make snap judgments in less than a second. Products and services have to display their trustworthiness quickly. They need to appear like they aren't going to rip us off, injure us, sell our personal data, break immediately, or otherwise betray our trust in them.

If we trust something, we are much more likely to deeply engage with it and perhaps even take measured risks with it. Would you rather walk across a sturdy steel bridge or a rotting, swaying rope one? A trustworthy product or service is one that users will take the time to examine and learn, discovering and using more features because they aren't afraid that something bad will happen to them if they do.

Appropriate

The solutions that interaction designers come up with need to be appropriate to the culture, situation, and context that they live in. All of these factors can drastically affect the type of product or service that a designer makes (**Figure 3.8**).

Figure 3.8

The henna decoration of this girl's hand could provide valuable insights for designers of products for India.

The Japanese and Koreans are famously advanced mobile phone users and can use expert features that would boggle Americans. In France, cooking and eating are social events best enjoyed slowly, and even simple meals are prepared with care; American-style fast food services have only grudgingly gained acceptance there after many years of struggle. Certain colors have different meanings in different cultures—for instance, white in China and Japan denotes mourning, whereas in Europe and America it denotes purity and cleanliness.

Dutch cultural anthropologist Geert Hofstede, in his book *Software of the Mind*, identified five major dimensions that can be used to help understand different cultures and adjust designs accordingly:

▶ **Power distance.** To what extent will members of a culture accept inequities in power among members of that culture?

▶ **Individualism versus collectivism.** Do members of a culture have loose ties to their families and others, or are they members of strong groups (especially families)?

▶ **Masculinity versus femininity.** How strong are the gender roles in a culture? In strong masculine cultures, traditional distinctions between the sexes are maintained.

▶   **Uncertainty avoidance.** How tolerant is a culture of ambiguity and uncertainty?

▶   **Long-term versus short-term orientation.** How much does a culture value the future over the past and present?

Where a culture places on these continuums can greatly affect design. For example, a culture that places a high value on uncertainty avoidance may prefer simple, limited choices in a product rather than many, complex ones.

An understanding of the specific situation that a product or service will work in, and also the emotional context of that situation, are essential to good design. Airport check-in kiosks (**Figure 3.9**) can't be complicated or require any significant learning to use them—they are used infrequently by harried people. Likewise, you wouldn't design a toy for young children the same way you would design a military communication device to be used in battlefield conditions. The situation dictates a set of constraints—technical, cultural, and emotional—that designers ignore at their peril.

Figure 3.9

An airport check-in kiosk like this one cannot be too complicated. It needs to take into account its context (a busy place) and the user's state of mind at the time of use (probably harried).

Smart

The products and services we use need to be smarter than we are. They have to prevent us from making mistakes or from working harder than we need to. They need to do for us humans the things we have trouble doing—rapidly perform computations, infallibly remember things over both the long and short term, and detect complicated patterns. They need to do the work we can't easily do alone. They have to be smart.

As noted earlier, Tesler's Law tells us that all processes have a core of complexity that cannot be overcome, only moved to different places. While taking care to not remove important skills from people, a good design moves as much complexity as possible into the services we use and the products we own, where it can be handled more effectively. Your mobile phone can hold far more phone numbers than you could ever memorize. Calling 911 will get the proper emergency services to your house more quickly than will looking up and then dialing the individual phone numbers. A Google search (**Figure 3.10**) will find obscure pieces of data more efficiently than will manually browsing because the Web service has taken on the complexity of browsing millions of pages.

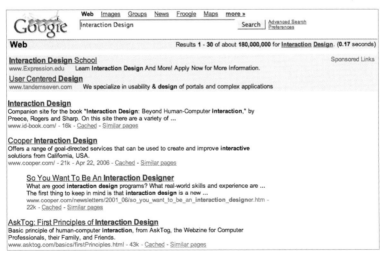

Figure 3.10

Google search results do what we cannot do ourselves: search millions of Web sites for specific words.

Responsive

As my wife will attest, there is little more annoying than talking to someone who doesn't respond. The same holds true for "conversations" with products and services. We need to know that the product "heard" what we told it to do and that it is working on that task. We also want to know what the product or service is doing. A spinning circle or a tiny hourglass icon doesn't give users much transparency into what is happening behind the scenes.

If a response to an action is going to take significant time (more than 1 second, which, believe it or not, can seem like a long wait), a good design provides some mechanism that lets the user know that the system has heard the request and is doing something (**Figure 3.11**). This doesn't make the waiting time less, but it makes it seem less. Excellent examples of such a mechanism are the indicators that tell you how long a process such as a software installation will take. These indicators also assure the user that the process hasn't gone into an endless cycle from which there is no return.

Figure 3.11

The Orbitz searching screen won't make the wait less for search results, but it will make it seem less because of its responsiveness.

The responsiveness of digital products can be characterized by these four basic levels, determined by the time between an action and the product's response:

▶   **Immediate.** When a product or service responds in 0.1 second or less, the user considers the response immediate and continues the task with no perceived interruption. When you push a key on your keyboard and a letter instantly appears, that is an immediate response.

▶   **Stammer.** If a product or service takes 0.1 second to 1 second to respond, users will notice a delay. If such a delay is not frequently repeated, users will probably overlook it. Repeated, it will make the product or service feel sluggish. For instance, if you press a key on your keyboard and it takes a second for the letter to appear on your screen, you'll notice the delay but likely will keep typing. If this happens with every key press, you will quickly become frustrated with your word processor.

▶   **Interruption.** After a second of no response, users will feel that the task they were doing was interrupted, and their focus will shift from the task at hand to the product or service itself. If you click a Submit button to execute a stock trade and nothing happens for several seconds, you will worry about the trade and wonder if the Web site is broken. Multiple interruptions can lead to a disruption.

▶   **Disruption.** If a delay of more than 10 seconds occurs, users will consider the task at hand completely disrupted. Feedback such as a progress bar or a timer that indicates how long a process will take will allay users' concerns and also allow the user to decide whether to continue the process. Marquees in the London Underground indicating when the next trains will arrive are excellent examples of responsiveness that addresses this level of delay.

Responsiveness makes people feel appreciated and understood.

Clever

Clever implies intelligence without smugness or condescension. It suggests humor and slyness without being obnoxious. And it also implies delight. Using a clever product or service, especially for the first time, leads to

Figure 3.12

TiVo's Instant Replay (or eight-second rewind) button is clever in that it anticipates users' needs (to hear or see the last bit of a show again).

moments of delight when you discover how clever, how thoughtful, it is. And delight is one of the most sublime emotions that one can experience, leading to long-lasting good feelings.

Clever products and services predict the needs of their users and then fulfill those needs in unexpectedly pleasing ways. TiVo is a particularly clever service. Its designers anticipated how users would enjoy the service and designed it with cleverness in mind. An excellent example of this sort of design is its eight-second rewind button. Often while watching TV, viewers will miss a line of dialogue ("What did he just say?"). Rewinding eight seconds is typically enough to hear the line again (**Figure 3.12**). The first time viewers use the clever eight-second rewind button, they typically are hooked on the feature.

Ludic

As children, we learn how to be adults through play. We play house. We role play adult authority figures. We learn teamwork through sports and group activities. Through play, we explore and experiment with life (**Figure 3.13**).

Figure 3.13

Two little girls playing doctor. Through play, we explore the unknown.

Ludic (pronounced "loo-dik") means playful. Designing products or services that allow play doesn't mean designing everything to be a toy or game, but rather providing the environment and means for users to play with a product or service. Through serious play, we seek out new products, services, and features and then try them to see how they work. How many times have you pushed a button just to see what it did?

It is hard to play when you are uncomfortable, so users need to be made to feel relaxed enough so they can engage in play. A well-designed product or service makes making errors difficult instead of simply providing lots of warning messages, which make people nervous and uncomfortable.

Play also requires a lack of serious consequences. While in a larger sense this feature may be difficult to design into medical devices, banking and emergency systems, and military applications, for instance, the ability to undo mistakes is crucial to fostering an environment for play. If the user feels trapped or powerless, the play is effectively over.

Pleasurable

Unless a product or service is pleasing to use, we likely won't use it often unless we have to (say, for our work or well being). In design terms, products and services can be pleasing in two ways: aesthetically and functionally (**Figure 3.14**).

As cognitive psychologist Don Norman pointed out in his book *Emotional Design*, beautiful products work better. Humans are more forgiving of mistakes in things that are more aesthetically pleasing. Objects that are agreeable to the eye or that fit well in the hand engender good feelings in their users, as do services in pleasing environments. The experience of eating at a fine restaurant is as often about the space and the other patrons as it is about the food.

Figure 3.14

A sauna is an enjoyable experience, not only because of the heat, but also because of the functionally and aesthetically pleasing wood that typically panels the room. If the room were tiled, the experience would be very different.

But beauty isn't everything. For a product or service to be appealing, it has to work well. Have you been to a beautiful Web site where you can't find anything? Products and services need to be functionally pleasing as well. We need to feel that time spent using the product or service is time well spent, that it is effective in accomplishing what we want it to do.

Summary

All of these characteristics, along with the laws and principles of interaction design, guide the products and services that interaction designers create. But we should never forget who these products and services are for: the users. So in the next chapter, we'll discuss how to talk to them, observe them, and make things with them.

4

Design Research and Brainstorming

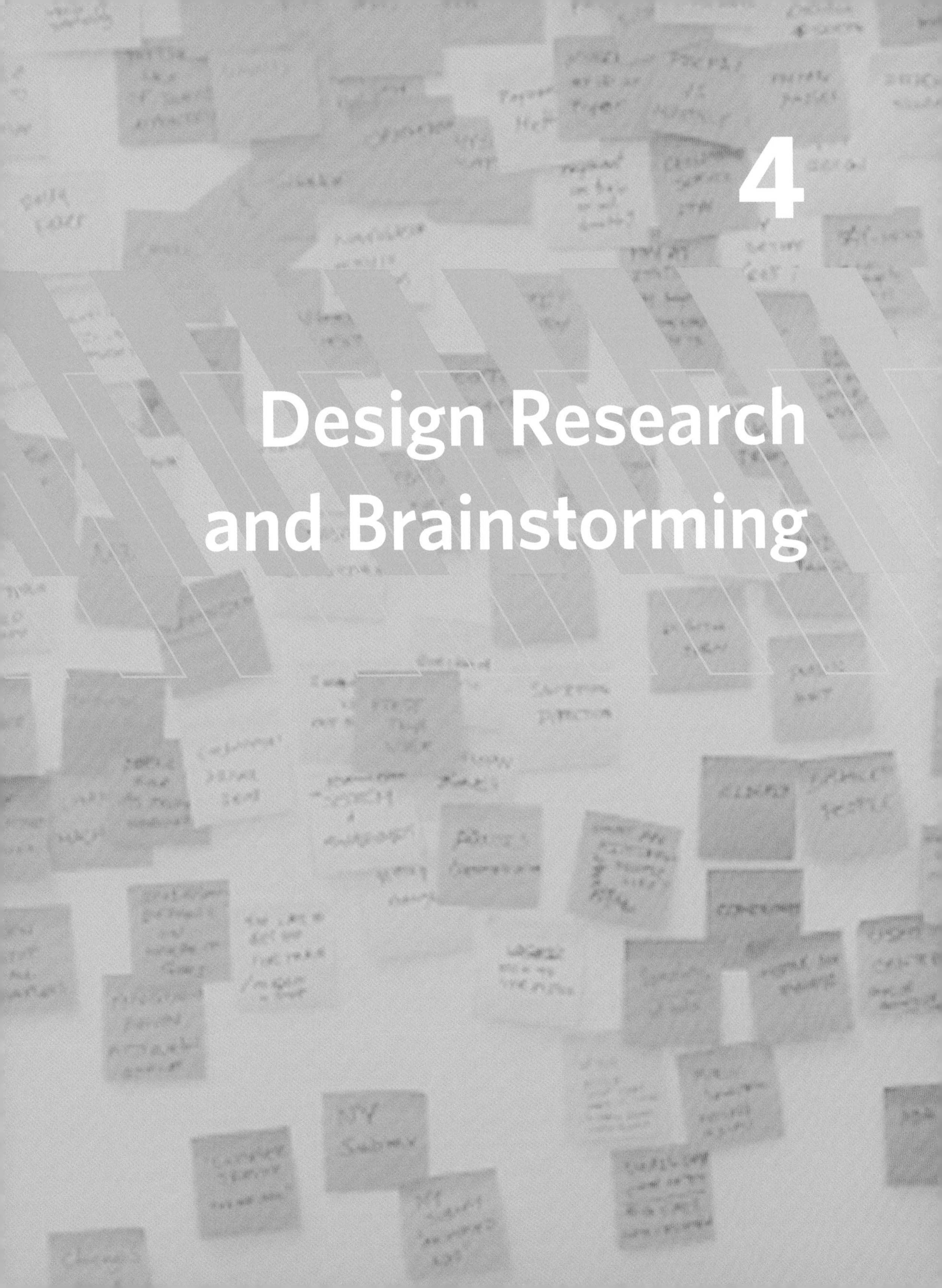

Imagine a zoo where the zookeepers don't know anything about animals, and they don't bother to find out about the animals' natural habitat, dietary needs, or natural predators. The zookeepers keep the animals in metal cages, group the animals randomly together, and feed them whatever they have around. Now imagine the chaos that ensues and the unhappy (or worse, sick or dead) animals that would be the result. Not the type of place you'd want to take your kids to.

Our fictional zoo is the state of a lot of the products and services today, albeit not so extreme. While most businesses do have strong interest in their customers and put considerable money into their products and services, a lot of that money is poorly spent. If only a small bit of the typical time, money, and resources used to make and market a product or service were spent on design research—observing, talking to, and maybe even making artifacts with customers and users—the products and services we use would be greatly improved.

What Is Design Research?

Design research is the act of investigating, through various means, a product or service's potential or existing users and environment. Design research uses a hodgepodge of methods drawn from anthropology, scientific and sociological research, theater, and design itself, among other disciplines. The methods (some of which I'll detail later in this chapter) range from silent observation to lively engagement with subjects in active play, such as role playing and model making.

Designers use these research methods to obtain information about the subjects and their environment that the designers otherwise may not know and are thus better able to design for those subjects and environments. It behooves designers to understand the emotional, cultural, and aesthetic context that the product or service will exist in. Only through research can designers find out.

Why Bother with Design Research?

Interaction designers aren't usually required to do design research. And as noted in Chapter 2, most designers don't; instead, they trust their instincts, knowledge, and experience to create useful, usable, and desirable products and services. In some cases, especially on small projects, this may be the correct approach. But on larger projects in unfamiliar domains, cultures, or subject areas, this approach can be lunacy.

Designers usually work on projects outside of their area of expertise (design), which most designers, being curious people, enjoy. (I've personally worked on projects for active stock traders, maintenance workers, teenagers, teachers, physically impaired elderly people, and news junkies, to name a few.) The only way, aside from being an intuitive genius, of understanding these diverse groups and the environments they live and work in is to do research. Meeting even a single user will likely change your perspective on a project. Spending a day observing someone do his or her job will give insights into that job that you would never get otherwise. Most designers will do some sort of research, even if it isn't formalized.

Brenda Laurel on Design Research

Brenda Laurel, Ph.D., is the chair of the Graduate Media Design Program of the Art Center College of Design as well as a Distinguished Engineer at Sun Microsystems. She has written and edited several seminal interaction design books, including Computers as Theatre, The Art of Human-Computer Interface Design, and, most recently, Design Research: Methods and Perspectives.

Why is design research important?

Perhaps the single most pernicious sort of folly I have seen over nearly thirty years in the computer field is the belief on the part of engineers, designers, and marketing people that they "just know" what will work for their audience. For an extremely observant, experienced designer, this may indeed be true, but such people are exceedingly rare, and those who are most successful have "trained" their intuition by carefully observing and reaching deep understanding of certain kinds of people, cultures, and contexts. For the rest of us, that first "great idea" is usually a shot in the dark. Examining the idea to discover the hypotheses that are implicit in it gives the designer a platform for inquiry that will inform the project. It may also surprise and delight the designer.

Brenda Laurel on Design Research Continued

Full-blown ideas for great, innovative products do not come from research subjects. The designer need not fear that engaging in research means that one is the slave of their findings. Design research includes the careful analysis of findings, turning them this way and that, looking for patterns. At the end of the day, well-designed research findings can spark the imagination of the designer with outcomes that could not have been dreamt of by either the research subjects or even the designer herself. Good design research functions as a springboard for the designer's creativity and values.

You've said that good design needs to understand "deep, roiling currents of our dynamic culture." Is research the best method for divining those currents?

Well, "research" is a pretty broad term. Exploration, investigation, looking around, finding out are all synonyms for research. In the business of cultural production, exposure to popular media is essential research. Television, movies, news, games, nonfiction, science fiction—all facets of the Spectacle—can provide a great deal of information about the trajectories of change, what people long for and what they fear; what sorts of stories are told and why; how people are likely to greet particular changes in their world.

What should designers look for when doing research?

The dictionary definition frames research as "scholarly or scientific investigation or inquiry." The first step is to deliberately identify one's own biases and beliefs about the subject of study and to "hang them at the door" so as to avoid self-fulfilling prophecies. One must then frame the research question and carefully identify the audiences, contexts, and research methods that are most likely to yield actionable results. Those last two words are the most important: actionable results. Often, the success of a research program hangs upon how the question is framed.

You've said that design needs to be a more "muscular" profession. How can research help in that?

Research helps design to become a more muscular profession because knowledge is power. Identifying the deepest needs of our times and carefully examining the complexes of beliefs, practices, attitudes, hopes, and fears that surround them can empower designers to do more than embroider the Spectacle. Muscular design can lift the veil and open new pathways through the challenges that confront us, from the everyday challenge of opening a bottle of medicine with arthritic hands to the global challenge of designing everything for sustainability, increasing delight while decreasing the weight of the human footprint on Earth.

Design research helps give designers *empathy* when designing. An understanding of the users and their environment helps designers avoid inappropriate choices that would frustrate, embarrass, confuse, or otherwise make a situation difficult for users.

Conducting Design Research

Anthropologist Rick E. Robinson has outlined three main rules drawn from anthropology for conducting design research:

- ▶ **You go to them.** Designers shouldn't read other people's research on their research subjects from the comfort of their offices. Designers shouldn't make subjects come to them, to an artificial testing environment in an unfamiliar location. Observing the environment—where activities are performed—is an essential component of any research.

- ▶ **You talk to them.** Designers shouldn't just read about their subjects. Nor should they only ask other people about them. Designers should have subjects tell their own stories in their own manner. The nuances of *how* a story is told can often tell a designer as much as the story itself.

- ▶ **You write stuff down.** The human memory is faulty. If designers can't write down what they see and hear directly as they do their research, then they should do so immediately afterward.

What Not to Do

Years of marketing methodology have left their mark on ideas about research. The first thing that most people think of when they think about talking to users is assembling a focus group. *Don't do this.* Focus groups are artificial constructs that, like juries, can be swayed and manipulated by strong participants, throwing off natural results. And that's to be expected— focus group facilitators assemble people into a synthetic group in an artificial setting (usually a conference room with a two-way mirror) and pepper them with scripted questions. This is not a good way to do design research. Rule #1: You go to them.

Nor is it a good idea to rely solely on the research of others, unless they are on the design team. Without knowing the circumstances and methods of the research, designers typically can't verify that the results are good and that they record the data that is most important to the designer: what the subjects did, said, or made and the environment they were in. This dictum is especially true for data derived from marketing research. Marketing research typically focuses on demographics and attitudes—some of the least interesting data from a designer's point of view. Rule #2: You talk to them—emphasis on *you*.

Designers shouldn't rely on a videotape or transcript to capture what they need to remember. Reviewing audio or videotape is a tedious process and will seldom be done, except to find specific moments. Transcripts of tapes, while useful, take time to create even when using a transcription service, and the designer may need the information before the transcript is complete. And there is always the possibility of that dreadful moment when the video camera doesn't record or malfunctions. Designers need to take their own research notes, both for safety and simply to focus their observations. Rule #3: You write stuff down.

Ethical Research

When conducting research, designers should strive to treat their subjects ethically. Not only is this the right thing to do, but it will yield better results, since the subjects will likely open up more if they know and feel that they (and their data) are being treated well. Ethical research requires following these guidelines:

▶   **Get informed consent from subjects.** The designer should tell the subject that he or she is conducting a research study and explain the purpose. The subject must understand what is going on and agree to participate, preferably in writing. With studies involving minors, parental or guardian approval in writing is a necessity. Exceptions to this guideline are observations in public spaces where it would be impossible or impractical to get consent from everyone in view.

▶   **Explain the risks and benefits of the study.** Some studies carry with them risks. The designer may hear or see something that the subject doesn't want him or her to. The presence of a designer could be dangerous or make certain tasks cumbersome. But the designer should also explain what he or she hopes will improve as a result of the study ("We're going to build a better system for tracking shipments of ball bearings"), both to reassure the subject and to ensure good research results.

▶ **Respect the subjects' privacy.** Never use subjects' real names or other data that might identify them. Blur or hide faces in photographs. This will ensure that anything that subjects do or say won't have personal repercussions for them.

▶ **Pay subjects for their time.** People's time is valuable, and people who give some of it to provide insights to designers should be paid for it, at least a token amount. This payment doesn't necessarily have to be cash, although it should have value to the subjects.

▶ **If asked, provide data and research results to subjects.** Some subjects will want to see what you have recorded and the outcomes of the research. Designers should respect these requests.

Costs and Time

One myth of design research is that it is expensive and time consuming. And while it can be—some rare design research projects cost millions of dollars and take place over years—most design research takes place over days or weeks and costs in the tens of thousands of dollars. It is time and money well spent.

The materials necessary for design research can be as simple as a notebook and a pen, or as complicated as specialized software and video-recording equipment. Ideally, a research team will have at least two of everything: two notebooks, two cameras (in case one breaks), four pens. The research team itself should consist of (at least) two people who can trade off interviewing/moderating duties during research sessions.

The amount of time spent doing research can vary widely but even a single day spent doing research will improve the outcome of the project. Ideally, however, designers will want enough time to interview and observe a representative group of users. In most cases, this will be more than 10 people, but fewer than 40. Time needs to be set aside not only for doing the research itself, but also for recruiting subjects, which can be quite time consuming itself. There are firms that, when given a set of criteria, will recruit research subjects. Often companies will have a list of customers to recruit from, and there are also ways to recruit users over the Web. However it is done, recruiting takes time. Generally speaking, most design research takes from a week to two months to execute from beginning to end.

What to Look For and How to Record It

When in the field, designers can get overwhelmed with the amount of data they are suddenly receiving. Often the designers are in a strange environment interacting with strangers. The newness of everything makes everything seem important. But the designer needs to focus on observing the things that are truly essential—namely, specific activities, the environment where activities take place, and the interactions among people that take place during activities.

Designers can help themselves focus by creating a *hunt statement*. A hunt statement is a tool for narrowing down what the designer is researching and why. Hunt statements typically take this form: I am going to research X so that I can do Y. X is often an activity, and Y is usually a project goal or subject area. Here's an example: I am going to research how civil engineers use PDAs on the job so that I can build a PDA for them. Hunt statements should be developed before doing research so that there is a purpose to each piece of research. The more specific the hunt statement, the better.

Patterns and Phenomena

In the field, the main thing a designer looks for are *patterns*. These can be patterns of behavior, patterns in stories, patterns of responses to a question—any action or idea that keeps recurring. The rules of thumb are these:

▸   See or hear it once, and it's a phenomenon. Write it down.

▸   See or hear it twice, and it's either a coincidence or a pattern emerging. Write it down.

▸   See it or hear it three times, and it's a pattern. Write it down.

Sometimes patterns won't emerge until after the research data has been analyzed. Sometimes a pattern is obvious in the midst of doing the research. Indeed, one good rule of thumb is that when you start noticing many patterns, you've likely done enough research to draw some meaningful conclusions.

Phenomena are particularly interesting to a designer as well. Unusual behaviors—especially unusual methods of working—can suggest directions that will benefit other people in their work. Say an accountant has created a different use for a spreadsheet; perhaps this approach can be built into the spreadsheet so that others can use it as well.

It's never a good idea to do research alone. Having a second pair of eyes, ears, and hands is immensely valuable for observing, listening, and recording, and for discussing and analyzing the research data afterwards. Two people observing the same phenomenon can draw (at least) two distinct conclusions from it, provided both saw it in the first place. Sometimes another person can be valuable simply to help capture the rich data being observed. Patterns can be subtle and easily missed.

Field Notes

Writing down observations and key phrases is essential. Paper notebooks are best and less distracting than laptops or PDAs, unless the environment is one where a notebook may be more conspicuous, such as in an office environment.

All field notes should start the same way: recording the name of the person doing the research and the day, time, and place where the research is taking place. These details are crucial, especially for reference later in the project when these items can provide cues for recalling details. ("Remember that woman in the diner? The one we talked to last Tuesday. What did she say again?") Although the designer may record subjects' names and other data to provide compensation, for instance, this data should be kept separately from field notes, which should use pseudonyms instead of real names to preserve the anonymity of the subjects. Another thing to leave out, no matter how tempting, are personal opinions about the subjects, the observed activities, or overheard conversations, such as "That person is an idiot." Doing otherwise is simply asking for trouble. Subjects, clients, and teammates may want to see the field notes, and showing bias in them is not only unprofessional, but bad research. Bias in research can't be helped, but it can (and should) be minimized.

It's a good idea, however, for the designer to have a separate area on the page to jot down thoughts and feelings that arise during the research sessions, including possible patterns. This should be a place to capture quick reflections or flashes of insight that can be explored more fully later.

Other findings that should be written down in the field notes are:

▶ Exact quotes with indications of emphasis and tone—Bob: "I sure do love these controls" (said sarcastically).

▶ Sketches of the location, annotated with comments and detail.

▶ The history, steps, and context of any activities.

Still pictures should be taken when and where feasible. Ideally, these will be printed, attached to the accompanying field notes, and annotated with captions or other notes.

Research Methods

Design research has many methods, drawn from other disciplines or created by designers over the years. These methods can be roughly divided into three categories: observations, interviews, and activities, including having subjects make things and self-report on their activities.

Whole books have been written on the methods of design research, so we will discuss only a representative sample here.

Observations

The easiest and possibly the most fruitful of all design research methods is simply observing what people are doing. Designers can covertly watch or interact with people or tag along with subjects to ask them questions about how and why they are doing what they are doing.

- ▶ **Fly on the wall.** Go to a location and unobtrusively observe what goes on there. For instance, a designer could go to a mall and watch how people shop.

- ▶ **Shadowing.** Follow subjects as they go about their routines. This technique usually requires permission, as the designer is following the subject throughout the day, recording what is done and said.

- ▶ **Contextual inquiry.** A variation on shadowing, contextual inquiry involves going to the subjects' location and asking questions about their behaviors, such as "Why are you doing that? Could you describe that to me?"

- ▶ **Undercover agent.** Observe people by interacting with them covertly. A designer who wants to know about a service can pretend to be a customer and use the service.

When conducting observations, dress not to impress. The point is to blend in with the environment so that the observer isn't the one being observed. Observers should wear neutral, nondescript clothing that is appropriate to the environment. The more observers look like they belong, the more they'll become part of the background. Bring props if necessary. Some environments require certain items for the observer to seem normal, such as a backpack in school settings, a hard-hat on construction sites, or a suit in a conservative office.

Observers should choose their locations wisely and be willing to change to another one if the original doesn't seem to be yielding good results. Observers should sit or stand in places where they can observe without being noticeable. It's best to be at an angle when observing subjects instead of directly in front or back of them, because an angle gives a clearer line of sight.

Camera phones are excellent for inconspicuously snapping photos in public spaces. Remember, however, that any such photos should be used in an ethical manner.

Interviews

It's amazing what you can find out if you just ask. Talking to people and hearing their stories is a great way to uncover attitudes and experiences— but designers do need to be careful: what people say they do and what they actually do are typically two very different things. Here are some methods for talking to users:

▶ **Directed storytelling.** Ask subjects to tell stories about specific times they performed an action or interacted with a product or service. Moments to ask about are the first time they performed an action or used a product ("Tell me about the first time you used the system to place an order"), a time when the product or service hasn't worked ("Can you describe a time when you couldn't do something you wanted to with your mobile phone?"), and a time when they did something new ("Why did you try to use the screwdriver to pry open the phone?").

▶ **Unfocus group.** A method from design firm IDEO, this approach turns the traditional focus group on its head. Instead of assembling a group of users in a room to talk about a subject or product, this method suggests assembling a group of experts in the field, hobbyists, artists, and others to explore the subject or product from different viewpoints. The purpose is not to get a typical user's perspective, but instead an atypical view of the subject.

▶ **Role playing.** With a willing group or individual, role playing different scenarios can draw out emotions and attitudes about a subject, product, or service in ways that can be very fresh ("I'm going to pretend I'm a customer and interact with you. Is that okay?").

▶ **Extreme-user interviews.** Another method from IDEO, in this approach the designer interviews people on the outer edge of the subject matter. For example, a designer working on an interactive TV project might interview a subject who doesn't own a TV.

▶ **Desk/purse/briefcase tour.** Ask subjects to give a tour of their desk or the contents of their purse or briefcase (**Figure 4.1**). How people use their desks and what they carry with them can reveal a lot about their personalities and work habits. Are they messy or neat? Organized or disorganized? Do they have special systems for working? Are there family pictures?

Figure 4.1

A desk tour can reveal how people structure their personal space to work.

When talking to subjects, it's best to have what the Buddhists call the "beginner's mind." Designers should be open and nonjudgmental and should not assume that they know the answer beforehand. Simple questions can reveal powerful answers. When possible, designers should avoid questions that can be answered with a yes or no; instead focus on drawing out stories and answers to how, what, and why questions.

Activities

A recent trend in design research calls for designers to not only observe and talk to users, but also to have them engage in an activity that involves making an artifact. This process allows designers to draw out emotions and understand how people think about a subject. Doing activities frees subjects' creativity and allows them to express themselves differently than they would in an interview. Here are some methods for making artifacts with subjects:

▶ **Collaging.** Using images and words, have subjects make a collage related to the product or service being researched (**Figure 4.2**). For a mobile phone project, for example, designers might have subjects make a collage on mobility. The collage images can come from magazines, the Web, or stock photographs and should contain a wide range of subjects and emotions. The same is true for the words. About 200 words, both positive and negative, should be printed on strips of paper for use. Subjects should have a way to write their own words as well.

Figure 4.2

Creating collages can give visual and verbal clues as to how subjects think and feel about a topic.

▸ **Modeling.** Using modeling clay, pipe cleaners, Styrofoam blocks, cardboard, glue, and other modeling tools, designers can have subjects design their version of a physical or even digital product. For example, a designer could have gamers design their ultimate game console or have air traffic controllers design an ideal set of controls.

▸ **Draw your experience.** Give subjects drawing materials and paper and tell them to draw their experience with a product or service (**Figure 4.3**). A project about e-mail, for example, might have subjects draw the life cycle of e-mail on their computers.

Figure 4.3

Drawing experiences can bring out subjects' hidden experiences and emotions.

An important part of having subjects make things is having them explain their choices after they are done (**Figure 4.4**). Otherwise, the designer may be left with a perplexing object and no way of understanding it. Ask, for instance, why a subject chose negative words in the collage or why a subject built the robot that way. However, for the best results, designers shouldn't tell subjects beforehand that they will be explaining their choices; this could inhibit them as they complete the activity.

Figure 4.4

An essential part of having subjects make artifacts is having the subjects explain their choices afterwards.

Making artifacts requires more advance preparation than other forms of research. Designers need to gather and choose the materials for making the artifacts as well as the tools to do so.

Self-Reporting

Another type of activity is self-reporting. In this approach, subjects, not the researcher, record their activities and thoughts, and the researcher then collects and analyzes these records after the subjects are done. Self-reporting is an excellent tool for longer studies in multiple locations, when it would be impractical to send designers to do all of the research in person. Self-reporting can also be good for documenting moments that subjects might be reluctant or embarrassed to present to a designer in person. Self-reporting methods include the following:

▶ **Journals.** Subjects keep a journal of particular activities. A classic example is the journals kept by the Nielsen families, who write down what they watch on TV for two weeks' time so that the Nielsen ratings can be compiled.

▶ **Beeper studies.** Subjects wear a beeper, which the designer sets off occasionally during the day. When the beeper goes off, the subjects record in a journal what they are doing at that time.

▶ **Photo/video journals.** Subjects are given cameras and told to document activities and their daily lives. Research on dining experiences, for instance, might ask subjects to document every time they cook or eat something.

Self-reporting requires a lot of time and effort from the subjects, so the subjects should be selected (and compensated) accordingly.

Design Implications

All the design research in the world is useless unless designers lay out the implications of the research. It's astounding how often this crucial step is overlooked.

At the end of any research period, designers will have an unstructured mass of data: in notes, in pictures, and in their heads. All this data is, frankly, useless (and perhaps worse than useless: overwhelming and confusing) unless it is distilled into information that the designer can use. The designer has to give shape and meaning to the data—that is, design the data.

The first task is to put all this data into some sort of order: in a spreadsheet, in a table, even (or especially) on sticky notes all over a giant board (**Figure 4.5**). The designer needs to cluster the data in meaningful ways, to give it form, so it can be thought about. One approach is to make a conceptual model of the data (see Chapter 5), but even looking at the data laid out in any sort of way should be enough for the designer to begin to draw design implications from it.

Figure 4.5

After gathering data, the next step is to cluster that data into meaningful chunks.

Let's say a designer is researching a new watch that sends and receives e-mail. As part of her research, she observed and recorded the moments when people most often glanced at their watches. In looking over her data, she discovers that the people she observed looked at their watches most often when they were late and in a hurry. What is the design implication of this data? Well, one implication might be that users first and foremost need to see the time on a watch/e-mail device, since they are usually glancing at the device in times of stress. Users also might like a device built to detect faster movement (hurrying) so as not to distract the wearer with incoming e-mail until the wearer slows down.

Or here's another example: A designer has been interviewing stereo aficionados about how they use their stereo systems. He finds that a large number of them are jazz aficionados as well. One design implication is that any new stereo system should be optimized for playing jazz, or have an option that allows such optimization.

Some of the design implications the designer will draw out of the data may seem simplistic ("The new mobile phone should fit in a pocket or purse"), but later in the process, these implications can offer a good check on what is being designed. Does the new product or service address all the design implications from the research?

Brainstorming: "And Then a Miracle Occurs..."

There is often a moment of panic once the research is done and the design implications have been teased out. Now the designer has to start digging in and actually designing *something*. An idea about what the product or service is going to be needs to appear. It's here, in this moment, that a miracle occurs (**Figure 4.6**).

As the cartoon wryly notes, this is a mysterious process. For some designers, the research and interviews have already started to suggest solutions to pursue. Others, however, may be clueless at this point about how to proceed. For the latter, it may be best to simply plunge into documenting their design (see Chapter 5) and wait for solutions to arise. But most designers live and design somewhere between these two examples. The solutions arise (or at least start) in periods of focused brainstorming.

When brainstorming, designers should have all the research and problem definition documents such as the design brief close at hand and in view (taped to walls perhaps) for reference and inspiration. The hunt statement, too, should be displayed for reference and consideration. Tools for writing and sketching quickly are essential: white boards, sticky notes, blank sheets of paper, pens, pencils, markers, and so on.

"I think you should be more
explicit here in step two."

Figure 4.6

*Cartoon by Sidney
Harris. © 2003 The
New Yorker Collection
from cartoonbank.com*

Start with a warm-up exercise. For instance, first dwell on the subject at hand in the broadest possible sense. For example, on a project to build a Web site for a museum, spend 10 minutes doing a word association game on what art is or what a museum is. Or do drawings based on famous artists. Or have all the people in the room talk about their best (or worst) experience at a museum. What the exercise is doesn't much matter: the point of the warm-up is to get brains, hands, and mouths engaged before starting to generate ideas.

Set aside a fixed amount of time for brainstorming—usually not more than two hours at any given stretch. During that time, try to generate as many ideas and variations on ideas as possible. Don't self-censor or censor others. Sometimes from even terrible ideas, great ideas can later spring.

Stay focused. Put stray thoughts or unrelated ideas into a "parking lot": a physical place in the room where those sorts of wayward ideas can be captured, but not discussed.

Don't spend a lot of time on any one idea. In the initial brainstorming sessions especially, the goal is to generate as many ideas as possible. Save going into depth on any one idea for later. For now, more is, indeed, more.

Use the whole room. Post things up on walls. Simply seeing all the ideas may generate connections between them or generate new ideas. Document what has been done. Take pictures of what gets drawn and put up. This information will be invaluable later.

Where do these ideas come from? From two places: invention (the creation of something wholly new through imagination) and reinvention (the combination of old forms into something new). The latter is far more common. It is always fruitful to ask, "What is this product or service like? What is it not like?" in the search for existing patterns and forms that can be used for the project at hand.

But it is also useful to explore the unknown, to take giant leaps of imagination. To do that requires changing *perspective*, or how you think about something. For example, stop thinking of a computer as a machine. Don't think of it as a thing at all (if you can). Think of it instead as an action. It is a rush though wires. Or a thrown punch. Now imagine a computer as a thought itself. Is it a jolt? A vision? A nightmare? Changing perspective allows us to toss out convention and gain a fresh look at the project at hand.

Summary

Design research and brainstorming are interaction design's secret sauce. Spending time observing, interviewing, and interacting with subjects and then drawing implications from that research fuel designers' empathy and imagination. That imagination is the heart of brainstorming, where invention and reinvention happen.

After research and brainstorming, designers need to document what they've learned and the design to be created. That is the subject of the next chapter.

5

The Craft of
Interaction Design

After defining the project, interviewing stakeholders, and conducting design research, interaction designers next make a series of models, diagrams, and documents. Indeed, this is how designers *design*. Many of these items are paper documents, but they can be physical or digital representations as well. Designers use these models and diagrams to demonstrate their skill, knowledge, and ideas as well as to visualize and analyze what they learned earlier in the design process.

There is a perennial debate about design documentation: how much do you need? Some designers suggest jumping straight into prototyping, saying that far too many documents are created. Others wouldn't dare proceed without most of these documents for fear that something important wasn't written down somewhere.

My answer is that designers need exactly as much documentation as it takes to execute the project well. If the designer's team responds well to use cases, then by all means the designer should produce them. If a client couldn't care less about a task analysis, the designer shouldn't perform one unless the designer personally finds it helpful.

The only reason for interaction designers to make the models and diagrams they do is to communicate their knowledge of and vision for a project. Research models show what was learned from the user research. Personas demonstrate an understanding of the audience. Use cases and task analyses outline what the product or service needs to accomplish. Mood boards, scenarios, storyboards, task flows, sketches, wireframes, and prototypes pull all the pieces together into a vision of what the final product or service will be. Testing makes sure that that vision is shared by the users.

If a document doesn't communicate anything useful, it is worthless—less than worthless, in fact, because it squanders the designer's time. Each model or diagram produced should take the project one step further toward completion. These design documents are at the heart of the craft of interaction design.

The Tools of the Trade

No digital tool has yet to replace the speed and flexibility of a pencil and a piece of paper or a marker and a whiteboard. Those, plus the talent and wisdom of the designer, are the true tools of the trade. Before designers spend time fiddling with any of the software described here, they should spend some time thinking and planning with pencil and paper or on a white-board. Before they use computers to straighten their lines and make every-thing presentable, designers should rough out what is going to be made. In short, they should design the design.

To make the documents described in this chapter, interaction designers need a working knowledge of several programs in addition to a word pro-cessing program:

- **Diagramming software.** Programs for making charts and diagrams. Microsoft Visio and OmniGraffle are the standards. Adobe InDesign also works well.

- **Drawing or illustration software.** Programs for making realistic mock-ups of services and products. This software will be used for creating storyboards and prototypes. Adobe Illustrator, Adobe Free-Hand, Adobe Photoshop, and CorelDRAW are all good choices.

- **Prototyping software.** The software used for prototyping, mainly for digital products. The particular program used will depend on the type of product that the designer is working on. A Web site will require different prototyping software than a physical product probably will. Some typical programs are Adobe Flash, Solidworks, and HTML edi-tors such as BBEdit and Adobe Dreamweaver.

- **Presentation software.** Programs that designers can use to present their work in front of large groups. Microsoft PowerPoint and Apple Keynote are the standards. Adobe Flash and Acrobat can also be used.

- **Conversion software.** Programs for creating materials in a format that most people can use. The people a designer deals with may not have the software that the designer is using, so files need to be con-verted to a readable format. There's really only one option: Adobe Acrobat. Acrobat can convert most files created by the other pro-grams described here to PDF format, which anyone should be able to read.

Research Models

The first models made by designers usually are visualizations of research findings. As discussed in Chapter 4, the designer should have gleaned

Figure 5.1

An example of a model derived from research. Most of the features of the intranet system being researched were unknown and unused, and those that were used were disliked.

design implications from the research data, but some research data—patterns usually—needs to be visualized to be easily (or better) understood.

For example, **Figure 5.1** was created from data collected by talking to users of an intranet. The data revealed that much of the intranet wasn't being used, even features that users said they wanted. Part of the reason these features were unused was because users didn't know they existed—they were buried in the system. The data also showed that most of the features the users did know about, they disliked. Most of what the users wanted in an intranet was unused or unknown or not in the system.

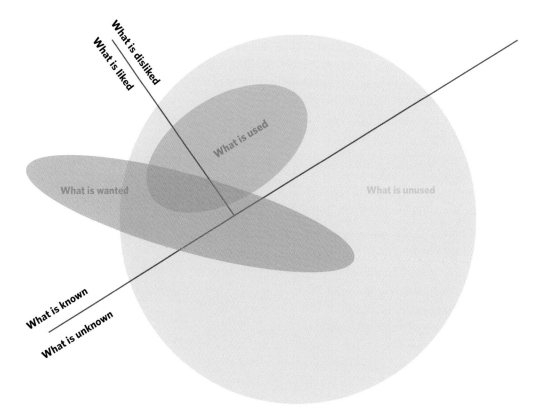

All of this information could, of course, be explained in words, as in the preceding paragraph, or shown in a statistical table. But neither of these has the same impact as the model. Models become design tools, to be referred to repeatedly throughout a project. In this example, the designers could easily see and demonstrate to the client that a key problem is that the users can't find the features they want to use, even when the features already exist in the system.

These are the most common tools for representing research data:

▶ **Linear flow.** Shows how a process unfolds over time (**Figure 5.2**). Linear flows are good for showing designers where problems exist in a process.

Figure 5.2

Linear process flow.

▶ **Circular flow.** Shows how a process repeats itself in a loop (**Figure 5.3**).

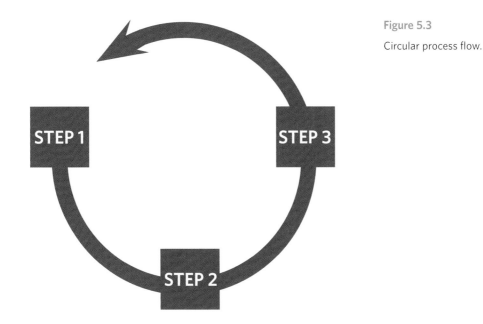

Figure 5.3

Circular process flow.

▶   **Spider diagram.** Shows connections between data points. A piece of
       data is placed in the center of a diagram, and other data radiates out
       from it (**Figure 5.4**).

Figure 5.4

Spider diagram.

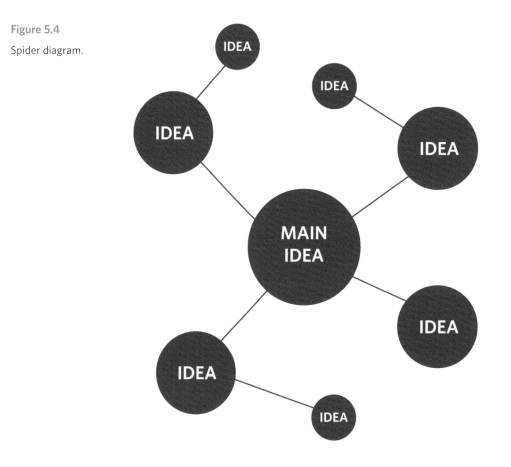

▶ **Venn diagram.** Uses overlapping circles to show relationships and sets (**Figure 5.5**; Figure 5.1 also is a Venn diagram).

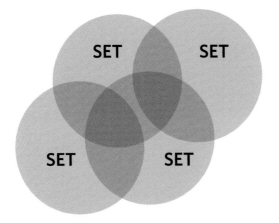

Figure 5.5

Venn diagram.

▶ **2x2 matrix.** Shows the relationship between data based on where the data points fall on two axes. These two axes separate data into four quadrants based on two simple variables (**Figure 5.6**).

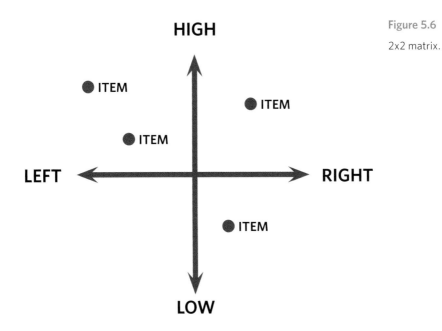

Figure 5.6

2x2 matrix.

▶   **Map.** Shows spatial relationships (**Figure 5.7**).

Figure 5.7

Map.

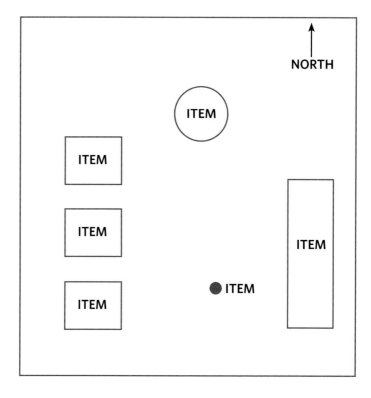

Often, the data itself suggests the correct way to display it. If, for example, the designer observes a step-by-step process that repeats, a circular flow makes sense to use.

Personas

Personas (**Figure 5.8**) are a documented set of archetypal people who are involved with a product or service. They're supposed to give designers a sense that they are designing for specific people, not just "the users," who, if ill-defined, can be twisted to serve any purpose. ("Of course the users will want to enter a password on every page!")

Dave
the information jockey
***primary* persona**

information usage
info Names, Phone Numbers, Ideas
paper Notebook, Post-Its
info access 3-5x/day
# of locations/day 5
% mobile 35
mobile locations Subway, Street

"If I'm not connected,
I feel like I'm missing
something."

demographics
age 29
occupation Lawyer
location New York City
marital status Single
children None
income $135,000
education Graduated Law School
hobbies Working Out, Cooking

device usage
computer Sony VIAO Laptop
cell phone Sony Ericcson
pda CLIE
other Network Walkman
primary device Laptop
comfort Comfortable
web 50 hours/week
phone 10 hours/week
programs Email, Word, Excel, IE

Figure 5.8

A sample persona. Personas turn "the users" into identifiable human beings.

Designers should devise personas from observing and talking to users. Personas are typically amalgams of multiple people who share similar goals, motivations, and behaviors. The differences between each persona must be based on these deep characteristics: what people do (actions or projected actions) and why people do them (goals and motivations).

What personas shouldn't be are users who have similar demographics. Focusing on demographics will provide market segments, not personas. The only time demographics really matter for personas is when those demographics directly affect user behavior. A 13-year-old will probably use a product differently than an 83-year-old. A rural peat farmer in Ireland might use a product differently than a Korean financial analyst in Seoul. But maybe not—demographics may not matter at all. In fact, using demographics could limit and hinder the usefulness of the personas. For products with millions of users, for example, a designer could end up with hundreds of personas, and such a large set is essentially useless.

To create a persona, designers find a common set of behaviors or motivations among the people they have researched. This set becomes the basis for the persona, which should be given a name, a picture, and a veneer of demographic data to make the persona seem like a real person.

For example, consider a design project related to airline travel. Designers have observed three sets of behavior: flying frequently for business, flying occasionally for pleasure, and flying habitually every fall and spring (the snow bird phenomenon). Each of these behaviors is tied to specific other behaviors while traveling, with different goals and motivations. The behaviors become the basis for three personas: Bob, the frequent flier; Susan, the vacationer; and Wilma, the snow bird.

Quotes pulled from the research are helpful for distinguishing and identifying personas ("I fly at least once a week"), as are simple titles ("The Frequent Flier"). The persona documents should clearly note the behaviors, motivations, and goals that differentiate one persona from another. Bob cares deeply about getting to his meeting or hotel on time, while Wilma is more relaxed about what happens after the flight.

For most projects, the number of personas should be small—anywhere from 1 to 7. After about 7 personas, remembering and distinguishing them becomes difficult (recall the Magical Number Seven rule from Chapter 3). Most important, it becomes difficult to design for such a large group. Imagine creating a mobile phone that will satisfy a dozen very different people. The debate that would go on among those people would make it difficult for the designer to accomplish anything. Unless you are designing for millions of users, you should consolidate personas to fewer than 7. While both designer and client will usually want the product or service to work for the largest possible group, 7 personas should be enough to cover 95 percent of the users. A product or service that is being designed to accommodate more personas likely isn't focused enough on the core behaviors that need to be addressed.

Once you have a set of personas, find a face for each. Pictures, more than anything else, will humanize personas and make them memorable. As long as the personas won't be made public, an online dating service like Yahoo Personals is an excellent place to find persona pictures. Personals contain (mostly) flattering pictures that can be browsed according to any combination of gender, location, age, ethnicity, and other factors.

Personas by themselves are fairly useless. They become useful only when the designer sets up scenarios and uses the personas to test features for appropriateness and utility. Designers can then ask themselves: Would this persona do this task? Could this persona do this task as it is designed?

Robert Reimann on Personas

Robert Reimann is President of the Interaction Design Association (IxDA) and Manager of User Experience at Bose Corporation. He helped write the book on interaction design—literally—with Alan Cooper: About Face 2.0: The Essentials of Interaction Design.

How did the idea of personas come about?

The idea of personas, or tools like them, has been around for a long time. Many design, marketing, and usability professionals in the 80s and 90s made use of "user profiles" to help them visualize who their customers were, and to help them imagine what kind of needs and desires they might have in relation to products and services.

Alan Cooper, who coined the term "persona" for this type of tool, first did so in 1983, while designing and developing a software package called SuperProject for Computer Associates, and later did so for what eventually became Microsoft's Visual Basic.

Cooper's early personas were "primitive," in that they were based on loose, personal observations of a small number of individuals in particular roles. However, Cooper's fundamental insight was that these representative characters had goals and behaviors that could be served by products. By enumerating the most critical goals and including them as part of the persona description, Cooper developed a powerful design method: meet the persona's top goals with the product by designing for their behaviors, and the design is much more likely to be successful.

My own contribution to Cooper's persona methodology was to introduce more formal ethnographic field research as the data-gathering method for the information used to construct personas, and to (with Kim Goodwin) refine the persona goals into three types: *experience goals*, which describe how users wish to feel (or not to feel) when using a product; *end goals*, which describe what users actually want or need to accomplish with a product to meet their expectations; and *life goals*, which describe the broader aspirations of the persona in relation to the product, and thus help describe what the product *means* to the persona. It's this focus on goals and behavior patterns, combined with a scenario-based method of translating these requirements into design solutions, that makes Cooper's personas so unique and powerful.

Robert Reimann on Personas *Continued*

What are personas good for?

Personas are terrific tools for understanding and communicating user behaviors, needs, desires, and contexts. They are extremely useful for:

1. Directing the product design. Persona goals and behaviors inform both the structure and behavior of a product and its interface.

2. Communicating design solutions to stakeholders. Using personas in storyboards and scenarios is a very effective way to tell the story of the product and helps highlight why design decisions were made as they were.

3. Building consensus and commitment around the design. Having a common language around which the team can communicate regarding priorities and features and tying each decision specifically to user benefits/consequences helps rally a team to work together to make the best possible product for its target users.

4. Measuring the design's effectiveness. Design choices can be tested against persona behaviors, contexts, and expectations while they are still on the whiteboard, far in advance of testing on prototypes or final products. The result is better quality earlier in the design process, which makes later refinements more manageable.

5. Contributing to nondevelopment efforts. The information captured in personas and storyboards can be of great interest and use to marketing, advertising, sales, and even strategic planning activities within companies.

What are the essential components of any persona?

The most important elements of any persona are the behavior patterns gathered via ethnographic research and analysis, and the goals that derive from them. Furthermore, it is important to understand each persona's priority as addressed in the design: for example, is it a primary persona (main design target), a secondary persona (served by an interface directed at the primary persona, but with some special additional requirements), or a persona that is not served by the product at all? In addition to these components, a representative name, a picture, and a small amount of additional demographic information help make the persona seem real and engage designer and stakeholder empathy. Personas must seem like credible, real people to maximize their effectiveness as design and development tools.

Designers (and, indeed, businesses) can also use personas to set priorities. The persona that represents a majority of a product's users may not be the user that the organization values the most; other personas may make the organization more money, be more involved, use more features, and so on. Organizations can and should use personas to make strategic decisions.

While many find personas helpful, some designers don't care for them. For these designers, personas form an artificial barrier between the product and its users. Some projects, especially smaller ones, may not warrant a full set of personas. But for many designers, if their personas are based on research and focused on the right characteristics (behaviors, motivations, and goals), personas are a valuable tool.

Scenarios

Scenarios provide a fast and effective way to imagine the design concepts in use. In a sense, scenarios are prototypes built of words.

Scenarios are, at their heart, simply stories—stories about what it will be like to use the product or service once it has been made. The protagonists of these stories are the personas. Using a scenario, designers can place their personas into a context and further bring them to life. Indeed, scenarios are one of the factors that make personas worth having. Running through the same scenario using different personas is an excellent technique for uncovering what needs to be included in the final product.

Consider an e-commerce Web site, for example. One persona is Juan, a very focused shopper who always knows exactly what he wants. Another persona is Angela, who likes to look around and compare items. If the designer imagines them in a scenario in which they are shopping for an item, the scenario starring Juan will have him using search tools, and the scenario starring Angela will have her using browsing tools.

One common scenario that works well for almost every product or service is one that imagines first-time use. What happens when the personas encounter the product or service for the first time? How do they know what to do and how to use the product or service? How does it feel to them? Running each persona through a first-time use scenario can reveal how to tailor the final design to appeal to and work for each persona.

A picture can be worth a thousand words, but a few words can also be worth quite a few pictures. Consider this example from a scenario for an online grocery delivery service:

Sarah logs onto her BigGrocery account. She sees her order from last week and decides to use it again for this week's order. She removes a few items by dragging them off her BigGroceryList. Her total cost adjusts appropriately. She has all the groceries she wants now, so she clicks the Deliver button. Her saved credit card account is charged, and her confirmation page tells her to expect the groceries in about an hour.

This scenario took only a few minutes to write, but it would have taken hours to storyboard, days to wireframe, and weeks to prototype. Using scenarios, designers can sketch with words.

Sketches and Models

Of course, designers can sketch with images as well as words (**Figure 5.9**). As stated earlier, the designer's best tool has been and continues to be the physical drawing surface (paper, whiteboard) and the physical drawing instrument (pencil, pen, crayon, marker). Nothing digital thus far has been able to match the flexibility, speed, and ease of sketching on a piece of paper or whiteboard. Space is just one reason—even the largest monitor cannot compete with wall-sized whiteboards or sheets of paper fastened together.

Another form of sketching is modeling. Models can be made of a variety of materials, from clay to cardboard to Styrofoam. Large blocks of Styrofoam can even be used to model physical spaces. Even crude blocks of wood, like those carried around by Jeff Hawkins to test the size, shape, and weight of the original Palm Pilot, can be models. Models, like sketches, can be rapidly put together in a short period of time to give rough approximations of physical objects and environments.

Sketching and modeling should be done throughout the design process, of course, but they are most helpful as visualizations of concepts and ideas that are still being formed to help to clarify and communicate those ideas and concepts.

Sketches and models are, by their nature, informal, and they can be easily changed. Viewers feel free to comment on them for just this very reason. This is a good thing, and no designer should feel overly attached to them.

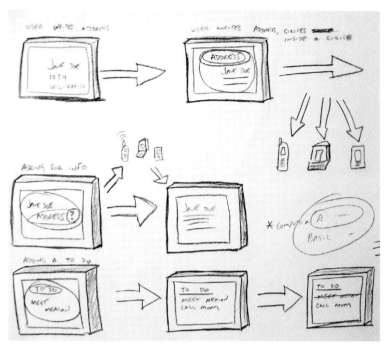

Figure 5.9

Sketching is an
essential design tool.

Storyboards

Once a scenario and sketches have been created to show what a product or
service could be like, designers can create a storyboard (**Figure 5.10**) to help
illustrate the product or service in use.

 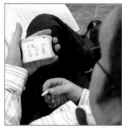 

Dave writes the word
Weather and circles it.

The page is replaced by the
local weather forecast.

After reading the page, Dave
draws an X across it and the
page disappears.

Figure 5.10

Storyboards illustrate
in words and images
what the experience
of a product or service
will be like.

Storyboarding is a technique drawn from filmmaking and advertising. Combining a narrative with accompanying images, designers can powerfully tell a story about a product or service, displaying its features in a context.

The images on a storyboard can be illustrations or staged photos created expressly for the storyboard (I don't recommend using generic or stock images, as they will come off as stilted and likely won't be specific enough to match the scenario). Storyboards consist of these image panels, with accompanying text that can be drawn directly from the scenarios.

Storyboards can also be used in conjunction with a wireframe (discussed later in this chapter) to illustrate the details of a complicated process or function. Using a storyboard, a designer can show key moments of an action. For example, a complicated drag-and-drop procedure could be shown with panels illustrating the first moment that the user picks up an object, what happens during dragging, and what happens when the object is dropped.

Task Analyses

A task analysis is a raw list of activities that the final design will have to support. A task analysis can be simple or very complex, depending on the project. For example, imagine designing a new Web browser. It's easy to create a list of major tasks. Users will need to be able to:

▶   Go to pages by manually entering an address.

▶   Go to pages via a bookmark.

▶   Add a bookmark.

▶   Delete a bookmark.

▶   Organize bookmarks into folders.

▶   Print pages.

▶   Refresh a page.

▶   Return to the previous page.

▶   And so on, all the way down to rare and obscure tasks (for most users), such as viewing page source code and opening a JavaScript console.

This list of tasks can be assembled from several places: from business requirements ("Users need to be able to contact customer service"), design research ("Everyone we spoke to said that a self-destruct button was essential"), existing products ("Every mobile phone needs to be able to make phone calls"), and especially from brainstorming and scenarios ("What if we gave users the ability to customize that display?").

Task analyses can be documented in spreadsheets or word documents. They can also be mapped to wireframes (discussed later) to indicate what tasks are being performed on each page. Tasks can be categorized by function, level of access required (basic user tasks, registered user tasks, administrator tasks, and so on), or even by the persona performing the task.

Task analysis is especially useful as a check to see whether the design supports all the tasks required. Rare but important tasks often get overlooked, but with a task analysis, the designer can make sure the design meets all the requirements.

Task Flows

Once the tasks have been established, putting those tasks into a sensible order, or flow, is an important step. Task flows (**Figure 5.11**) show the logical connections that will be built into wireframes (discussed later in this chapter). You can't, for instance, use the Back button on your Web browser to go back to a previous page until you've been to more than one page. You can't dial a mobile phone until you've entered a number. You can't change your preferences until you've registered. And so on.

Putting tasks into flows helps the designer begin to see the product take shape. Task flows can suggest page order on a Web site or in a wizard. Since task flows show when users will have to perform certain actions, they help clarify the implementation of controls (see Chapter 6). And when decisions have to be made, flows show where menus and information (or affordances) will have to be included.

Figure 5.11

Task flows like this one show the logical connections between actions.

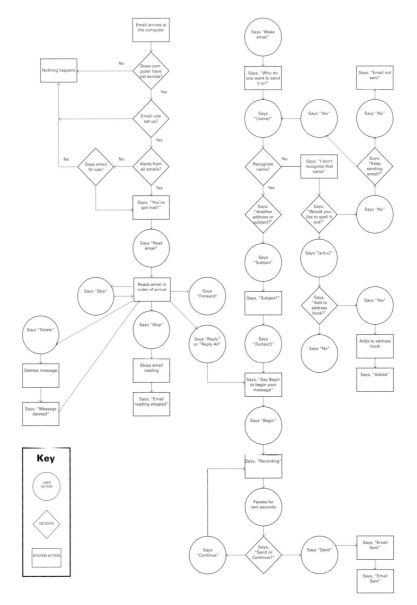

Use Cases

Programmers have used use cases in the design of software for years. Indeed, it is this tradition that gives use cases some of their power: developers are very accustomed to seeing them and will likely understand them immediately, as will the business people who have over the years had to use them to communicate with programmers. Other design documents, while gaining recognition and acceptance, are simply not as well established.

Use cases are a means of roughing out the functionality of a product or service. A use case attempts to explain in plain language what a certain function does and why.

Use cases also describe whom the function involves. Use cases begin by identifying a set of potential actors. These actors can be based on the personas, but they can even be simpler than that. For example, "the user" can be one of these actors. Another of these actors is typically "the system." The system is the generic actor for any automatic or computing process. It is typically these processes that programmers have been interested in defining, but use cases don't need to be limited to describing events involving the system.

Use cases have the following form:

▶ **A title.** This should be descriptive, since it will be referenced often, both in documents and conversation. For example, a use case from an e-mail project might be called "Send an E-mail."

▶ **The actors.** Who is performing the function? In the Send an E-mail example, the actors are the user and the system.

▶ **The purpose.** What is this use case meant to accomplish and why? For the function sending an e-mail, the purpose would be something like this: "An actor wants to send a message to someone electronically."

▶ **The initial condition.** What is happening when the use case starts? In our example, it is simply that the e-mail client is open.

▶ **The terminal condition**. What will happen once the use case ends? In the e-mail example, the condition is again simple: an e-mail will be sent.

▶ **The primary steps.** Discrete moments in this piece of functionality. In the e-mail example, these would be the steps:

1. Actor opens up a new mail window.

2. Actor enters the e-mail address of the recipient or selects it from the address book.

3. Actor enters a subject.

4. Actor enters message.

5. Actor sends mail via some method (for example, a button click).

6. The system checks to make sure the mail has a recipient address.

7. The system closes the mail window.

8. The system sends the mail.

9. The system puts a copy of the mail into the Sent Mail folder.

▶ **Alternatives.** Alternatives are other use cases that may consider the same or similar functionality. In the Send an E-mail example, Reply to Sender and Forward Mail might be use case alternatives.

▶ **Other use cases used.** Frequently, one piece of functionality is built upon another. List those for reference. The e-mail example includes a few functions that could have their own use cases: Open an E-mail Window, Select an Address from the Address Book, and Confirm Recipient Address might all be separate use cases.

Use cases can be broad (Send an E-mail) or very detailed (Confirm Recipient Address). Use cases can also be very time consuming to create, and a complicated system could potentially have dozens, if not hundreds, of use cases. Use cases are, however, an excellent tool for breaking down tasks and showing what the system will have to support.

Mood Boards

Mood boards (**Figure 5.12**) are a means for the designer to explore the emotional landscape of a product or service. Using images, words, colors, typography, and any other means available, the designer crafts a collage that attempts to convey what the final design will feel like. Images and words can be found in magazines and newspapers or online image galleries, or can be created by the designer. Some designers take and use their own photographs for mood boards.

Figure 5.12

A mood board explores the emotional landscape of a product or service.

Traditionally, mood boards were made on large sheets of poster board (thus, the name). The advantage of this approach was that the result could be posted on a wall to be glanced at frequently for inspiration. But this doesn't need to be so. Mood boards can be created digitally: as animations, movies, screen savers, or projections on a wall. The advantage of digital mood boards is that they can include movement and sounds—something traditional paper mood boards obviously cannot do.

The important point is that whatever form the mood board takes, it should reflect *on an emotional level* the feeling the designer is striving for in the product or service. The mood board shouldn't be challenging intellectually; like a good poem or piece of art, it should affect viewers viscerally.

Wireframes

Wireframes (**Figure 5.13**) are a set of documents that show structure, information hierarchy, functionality, and content. They have their roots in architectural drawings and network schematics (in fact, they are sometimes called schematics). Other than prototypes, wireframes are the most important document that interaction designers produce when working on products. (Services don't typically have wireframes. Instead they have service blueprints; see Chapter 8.) Wireframes are a means of documenting the features of a product, as well as the technical and business logic that went into those features, with only a veneer of visual design (mostly just the controls of the product). They are the blueprints of a product. Developers, industrial designers, copywriters, and business people use wireframes to understand and build the product in a thoughtful way without being distracted by the visual or physical form.

Figure 5.13

Wireframes show the structural and functional elements of a product, devoid of visual and industrial design.

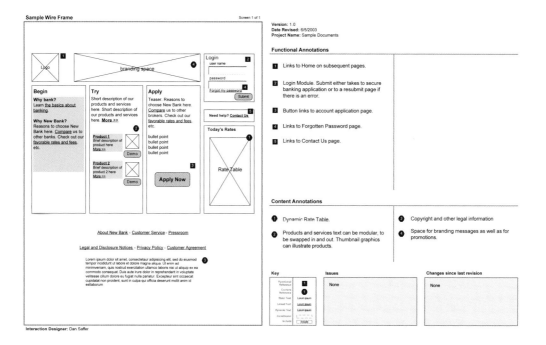

Wireframes are tricky documents to create because of the multiple audiences that read and use them. Clients want to see how the design meets their business goals. Developers want to see how the product works (and doesn't work—for instance, what happens when an error occurs) so they can know what they need to code. Visual or industrial designers want to see what visual or physical elements will need to be designed, such as the number and type of buttons. Copywriters want to see what they need to write: help text, manuals, headlines, and so on. And designers want to be able to refer to them in the future to remember details such as why there are two buttons instead of one for a certain feature. Accommodating the needs of these various audiences in one document is the designer's task. The wireframe, like all models and diagrams, is really a communication device.

Wireframes typically have three main areas: the wireframe itself, the accompanying annotations, and information about the wireframe (wireframe metadata).

The Wireframe

The wireframe itself is a detailed view of a particular part of a product. Wireframes can show anything from an overview of a product—the face of a PDA, for instance—to detailed documentation of a particular functionality, such as the volume control on a music editing application.

Wireframes should rough out the form of a product. Form is shaped by three factors: the content, the functionality ("form follows function"), and the means of accessing or navigating to those two things. Thus, the wireframe needs to include placeholders for the content and functions as well as the elements for navigating them (buttons, switches, menus, keystrokes, and so on).

Content is a deliberately vague term that includes text, movies, images, icons, animations, and more. Text, unless it is specifically known or being suggested by the designer (for instance, a button label), is typically represented on wireframes by greeked or dummy text. This dummy text is often the one used by typesetters since the 1500s: *Lorem ipsum dolor sit amet, consectetur adipisicing elit, sed do eiusmod tempor incididunt ut labore et dolore magna aliqua.* It's become somewhat of a tradition to use it in wireframes. Other content items are usually represented by boxes with Xs through them and some indicator of what they are, either on the wireframe (preferable) or in the annotations.

Functionality consists of the controls—the buttons, knobs, sliders, dials, input boxes, and so on—of a feature, as well as the product's feedback to those controls. A simple Web site form, for example, usually consists of labels ("Enter your name"), text boxes (where you enter your name, for instance), radio buttons ("Male? Female?"), check boxes ("Check here to join our mailing list!"), a Submit button, a Cancel button, and error messages ("You forgot to enter your name!"). All of these need to be documented on the wireframe.

There also needs to be a way to find and use the content and functionality: navigation. Navigation can consist of any number of methods, such as hyperlinks, simple drop-down menus, toolbars with widgets, and complex manipulations in physical space. On some mobile phones, for instance, pushing the cursor key down while pressing the star key locks the phone. On a digital camera, to view the content (the pictures that were taken), the user may have to change the mode of the camera and then use buttons to flip through the photos.

All these components should appear on the wireframe in a way that shows their general placement and importance. Note that the same wireframe can be used to design many different forms; wireframes can be interpreted in different ways by the visual or industrial designer. What is important is that all the items (content placeholders, functionality, and navigation) needed to create the final product be on the wireframes.

Anything on a wireframe that is not obvious or labeled should have a corresponding annotation.

Annotations

Annotations are brief notes that describe nonobvious items on the wireframe. They explain the wireframe when the designer isn't there to do so. When developers or clients want to know the reason for a button, they should be able to read the annotation and understand not just what the button does, but also *why* the button is there. Documenting "why" is a challenge, since annotations should be brief. But there is a vast difference between an annotation that says, "This button stops the process," and one that says, "This button stops the process so users don't have to wait for long periods." In the second version, the reader immediately knows the reason for the button. If a change occurs in the process ("The process now takes only a second"), it's easier to see how to adjust the design appropriately.

Here is a partial list of wireframe objects that should be annotated:

▶ **Controls.** (See Chapter 6 for a list of controls.) What happens when a button is pushed or a dial is turned or a hyperlink is clicked.

▶ **Conditional items.** Objects that change based on context. For example, in many application menus, certain items are dimmed depending on what the user is doing at the time.

▶ **Constraints.** Anything with a business, legal, logical, or technical constraint (for example, the longest possible length of a password or the legal reason that minors cannot view certain content).

▶ Anything that, due to space, could not be shown in the wireframe itself (for example, every item on a long drop-down menu).

Wireframe Metadata

Each wireframe should have information about that wireframe—that is, wireframe metadata. Every wireframe should include the following:

▶ **The designer's name.**

▶ **The date the wireframe was made or changed.**

▶ **The version number.**

▶ **What has changed since the last version.** Clients like this; it shows that the designer is actively addressing issues that have arisen during the project.

▶ **Related documentation.** Any related documentation (ideally with a specific page number) that is relevant to this wireframe: business requirements, technical specifications, use cases, and so on. If there are questions about the wireframe ("Did we really say that the robot wouldn't swim?"), appropriate documents can be referenced.

▶ **Unresolved issues.** Are there problems with the wireframe that still need to be addressed?

▶ **A place for general notes.** This is the place for the designer to express any final reservations about the product—especially the constraints that affected it. I have occasionally noted where business or technical constraints have had a negative impact on a product and should be addressed. In this way, designers can either argue for changes upon presenting the wireframes, or, if the clients or developers are reluctant to change the constraints, bring them up in the future when complaints arise or another version is planned.

Prototypes: Paper, Interactive, and Physical

The final, essential step before a product or service is launched or, ideally, tested with users is the creation of a prototype—or, even better, multiple prototypes. Prototyping is where, finally, all the pieces of the design come together in a holistic unit. Indeed, many clients will have difficulty understanding a design until they see and use the prototype. Like all the other models and diagrams, it is a tool for communicating. Prototypes communicate the message "This is what it could be like."

What form these prototypes take depends on both the designer's resources and the type of product or service that is being designed. A designer with the right resources can produce some high-fidelity prototypes that look and behave just like the final product or service would. Many retail chains build whole prototype stores!

The purpose of all prototypes is to explore some characteristic of the final product or service. Perhaps one of the prototypes is efficient and bland; another is more whimsical and approachable. One is menu-driven; another uses more direct manipulation. One prototype uses sliders; another uses dials. Designers use prototypes to experiment and see what works—for the designer, for clients, and for users. Frequently, one prototype is clearly the right approach, but just as often, after testing, it becomes clear that parts of each prototype work well, and the designer has to shape these into another prototype that is a hybrid of the best of the earlier prototypes.

Most interaction designers work with three types of prototype: paper, digital, and physical. We'll discuss each in turn.

Paper prototypes (**Figure 5.14**) are usually the fastest to create to demonstrate a working product or service. On paper, the designer creates a walkthrough of the product or system. Each piece of paper contains one moment of the design. That moment can be a Web page, a screen, or a part of a service. Viewers can step through the prototype by flipping through the pages in a particular order. Pages should be numbered, and instructions for moving between the pages should be provided ("If you press this button, go to page 9"). During testing (described in the next section), the subjects or the designer can write comments and notes directly on the prototype ("I really want this button to be *here*"). Another advantage of paper prototypes is that they are obviously not the final product, so viewers (and designers) subconsciously feel that they are more malleable.

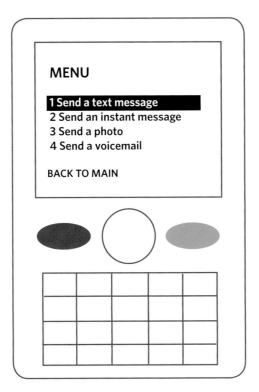

Figure 5.14

Paper prototypes like
this one allow subjects
to make comments
directly on the
prototype.

Digital prototypes (**Figure 5.15**) can take many forms, from static images to complex, 3D flythroughs of a service that are like Hollywood movies. Digital prototypes can have very limited functionality—users can click through images in the same way that they turn pieces of paper in paper prototypes—or they can be highly functional, with users being able to interact with the system and the system responding just as it would in the final product. For complex functionality, the richer and more complete a designer can make the digital prototype, the better. It is hard for prototype viewers to imagine how, for instance, a tool to draw boxes might work without being able to play with it, drawing boxes themselves. The danger with a high-fidelity prototype is that both users and clients may think it is the final product. Once a visual design is added, most will want to comment and focus on that instead of the functionality.

Figure 5.15

Digital prototypes can be easily distributed over the Web.

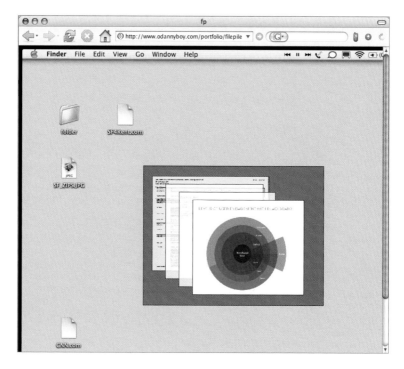

One advantage that digital prototypes have over other forms of prototypes is that they are easily distributed. Designers can put them on the Web or send them out on disks and have users play with them wherever they are. For software or Web sites, this means that users experience them on their own machines, in their own environments, as they would the final design.

Physical prototypes (**Figure 5.16**) can be made for simple parts of a design (such as a dial or a button) or, for services, they can be complete physical environments that are like theatrical sets. As with other prototypes, the level of fidelity can vary greatly. Physical spaces can be created exactly so that users think they are really in the location, or images can be projected on a wall to simulate the location. A device can be made with the exact materials it will eventually be made of (plastic and metal, for instance), or it can be approximated with materials such as wood or clay.

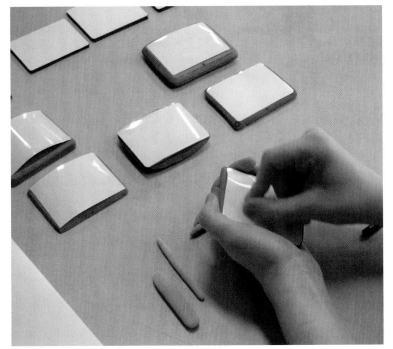

Figure 5.16

Figure 5.16

A physical prototype can be as small as a control or as large as whole rooms.

Prototypes are the ultimate expression of the interaction designer's vision. Indeed, many designers feel that prototyping is *the* design activity, that everything before it is but a prelude, and that to design *is* to prototype. The importance of prototypes cannot be overestimated.

Testing

Once you have a prototype, a logical audience for it is its intended users—the product or service should be tested with users. This process is usually called user testing, but that's really a misnomer; it's the product or service that's being tested, not the users (**Figure 5.17**).

Figure 5.17

A digital prototype
is tested by a user
at home.

The same rules that guide design research (see Chapter 4) also guide testing: you go to the users, you talk to them, you write things down. Unless what is being tested is a service that requires a prototyped space or some other significant setup, testing is best done in the subject's own environment: on the subject's computer, in the subject's home or office, in the subject's city or town. Testing labs have only one advantage: efficiency. The designer can quickly see many subjects in a single day, one after the other, without having to change location, and there is only one setup.

Testing is also the time when any wrong conclusions reached during design research can be corrected. Designers may find that they drew the wrong implications from the research. By talking to users during testing, those misconceptions can be cleared up. Ideally, designers will carry a set of wireframes and other documents during testing and make notes right there about any patterns they see. For example, if users keep stumbling while attempting to complete a registration form, the designer should plan to revise that form later.

Designers, when testing, should not be defensive about their designs; indeed, it is often best if designers allow other team members or usability specialists to conduct the testing while they simply observe and take notes—for the designer to be present, but not guiding. The human tendency is to nudge subjects ("Why don't you just look over there at that button?") because the designer knows the design better than the subject. To avoid inhibiting testers, designers should avoid identifying themselves as the product's designer. Knowing that the designer is present may cause testers to change or soften their feedback.

Most experienced designers know one truism: you seldom get it right the first time. Testing will reveal the flaws, both known and unknown. Nothing is more humbling for designers than watching users stumble through their designs. While testing, good designers watch for the same thing they watched for in design research: patterns. Then they go back to the wireframes and prototypes and fix the errors. Then they test them again. This is how products and services should be made.

Summary

The craft of interaction design is really the craft of creating the models, diagrams, and documents that communicate the designer's designs. These representations, and the testing of those with clients and users, are the designer's bread and butter. They are what designers use to do their most important work, moving their knowledge and vision from their minds and hearts to their hands and to the design itself. Designing, as Hillman Curtis has noted, is making the invisible visible, and this is what the best models, diagrams, and documents do. The quality of the models and diagrams and documents that designers make reflects the quality of the designer. Designers should strive to make each representation a designed artifact, filled with smart, deliberate choices.

6

Interface
Design Basics

We can engage with digital products only through some sort of interface. We can't (yet) connect to digital devices through a cable directly from our brains to their microprocessors. For now, we need some intermediary to communicate between us and our digital devices: an interface.

Interface design is so closely tied to interaction design that many believe they are the same thing, which isn't exactly true. Interface design is only the *experienced representation* of the interaction design, not the interaction design itself. The interface is only what people see, hear, or feel, and while it is immensely important, it is only a part of interaction design.

Interfaces are a bit like icebergs. The part that can be seen is really just the tip; what's below the surface, what isn't seen, is the main part of the interaction design: the design decisions that the designer has made and the technical underpinnings that makes the interface a reality. An interface is where the interaction designer's choices about how people can engage with a product and how that product should respond are realized. In other words, the interface is where the invisible functionality of a product is made visible and can be accessed and used.

This is not to say that interaction designers should ignore or downplay the interface. Not at all. If an interface doesn't display the attributes of good interaction design as described in Chapter 3—trustworthy, appropriate, smart, responsive, clever, ludic, and pleasurable—users aren't going to engage with it. All the time the interaction designer spent crafting rich functionality will be for naught if the interface is poor.

In the past, form closely followed function. A hammer looks the way it does because its shape is optimal for driving in nails. With digital devices, however, form doesn't necessarily follow function. Objects on a screen can have any shape and can potentially serve any purpose. For example, an unlabeled button sitting in the middle of a Web page could look like an elephant, a tea cup, or even like, well, a button, and clicking it could open another Web page, start an animation, play music, close the browser window, or do a variety of other things. When working with digital devices, the interaction designer has a lot more fluidity and ambiguity to account for.

Remember too that interaction designers also design services, where the interface typically consists of physical spaces, products, and people (see Chapter 8).

The Elements of Visual Interface Design

Interaction designers mostly create interfaces that are visual or at least have some visual component. Visual interface components include buttons, labels, the position of items on a screen, the position of the screen on the device, and a host of other interaction design elements.

Unlike the visual and industrial designers they often work alongside, interaction designers are typically less concerned about branding and pure aesthetic elements than they are about the controls and responses of the product—how the interface affects the interaction design—and those are the elements of visual interface design that we'll focus on here.

Visual interfaces consist, essentially, of only a handful of elements. The way those elements work together is what defines the visual interface.

Layout

At the core of all screen (and print, of course) visual design is *layout*: where and how the features, controls, and content are placed. Layout provides the structure that these elements reside within. Layout provides hierarchy, letting users know what is important and what is less so—a control that is visible at all times is perceived as more important than one that is buried in a drop-down menu. Layout is particularly important for small screens, since screen real estate is at a premium.

Grid Systems

Designers can seldom go wrong starting with a grid system (**Figure 6.1**). A grid system helps designers organize information into a coherent pattern. Designers start by dividing the screen into basic, rational chunks, including *gutters*, which are the blank spaces that separate rows and columns. Designers can let elements such as images, toolbars, and working spaces cross over gutters when necessary, creating larger blocks of combined rows and/or columns. The grid lines are only suggestions, not rigid areas. Grid systems aren't just designs on graph paper; done well, they help structure screens so that there is a clear visual hierarchy and flow through the elements on the screen.

Figure 6.1

Grid systems help designers organize information into a coherent pattern. Note the *gutters*: the blank spaces that separate rows and columns.

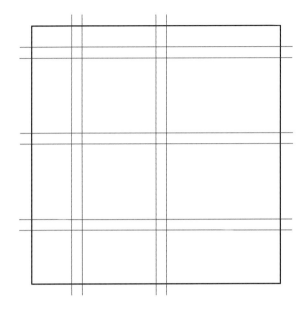

Several grid systems have become standards in interface design. **Figure 6.2** shows a typical layout seen in applications such as Microsoft's PowerPoint and Apple's iTunes: a thin, left panel and a large central window, along with top and bottom rows.

Figure 6.2

A grid system seen in such applications such as PowerPoint and iTunes. Top and left panels are used for controls or navigation, while a large central panel is the work area.

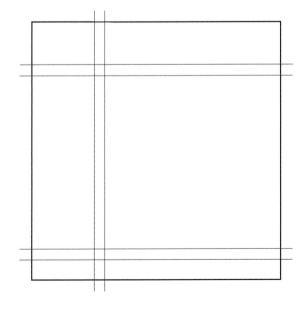

Figure 6.3 shows another familiar grid, used frequently in e-mail clients and RSS readers: a thin, left panel with two panels on top of each other on the right.

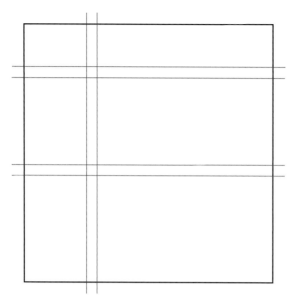

Figure 6.3

A grid system used in e-mail and RSS clients. The large right panels are used for displaying multiple items such as a list of e-mail in the top pane, and a more detailed view such as a single e-mail in the bottom pane.

Figure 6.4 shows a common three-column Web site grid.

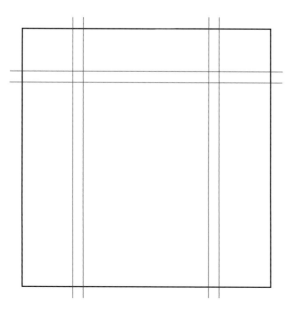

Figure 6.4

A grid system frequently used by Web sites. Navigation features or a banner is in the top row, while content, advertising, and other navigation features are in the bottom columns.

Even applications that seem freeform like Internet Explorer and the simple screens of mobile phones can be designed using a very simple grid system (**Figure 6.5**) that contains only a thin row at the top for a menu bar or tools such as a battery-life indicator, and a larger display or working space below.

Figure 6.5

A simple grid system used as the main screen in many applications. The top panel is for menus and/or icons, and the bottom area is a working space.

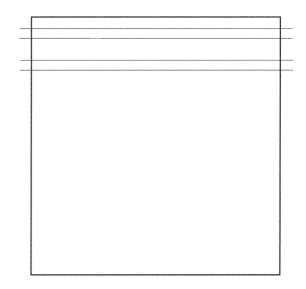

One thing that grid systems do well is help designers plan *whitespace* in the visual design. Whitespace is an area of blank screen that separates one filled area from another. A common mistake of interaction designers is to cram as many features onto a screen as possible, creating a very cluttered screen. Clutter creates visual noise and makes an application hard to use. The eye bounces from one thing to another, without seeing a clear flow and distinct parts of the screen. Whitespace between features will create a cleaner, clearer design.

Another reason not to cram too much onto a screen is that when objects are close together, Gestalt psychology tells us, the mind will assume that they are related. This is a good thing when designers want objects to seem related—for instance, a Submit button next to a text box—but not so good when the pieces of functionality drifting into each other are unrelated.

Visual Flow

Visual flow can be achieved in a number of ways, including by the use of the aforementioned whitespace. In the Western world, the eye generally travels from left to right, top to bottom, and designers should be aware of this flow and design for it. Don't force users' eyes to jump all over the screen.

Designers need to provide cues regarding where the user should look. Color (discussed later in the chapter) can be used to attract the eye, as can contrasting fonts (larger, bold, and so on). Lines and boxes can group objects together, but these should be used sparingly, lest the users focus on the lines and boxes and not the features—try to use whitespace instead.

Positioning and alignment of objects are also important. Objects that are aligned (**Figure 6.6**) will appear to be related, and objects should ideally be aligned horizontally and vertically to create a clean look. Objects that are indented beneath other objects (**Figure 6.7**) will appear to be subordinate to those above them, and objects near the top of the screen will generally seem more important than those farther down.

Designers should always perform the squint test on their visual interfaces. By squinting at the screen, designers can manually smudge the details and see which items on the screen have prominence. This test can often lead to surprise, revealing that secondary or unimportant items seem overly important in the design. The squint test helps ensure that the layout is strong.

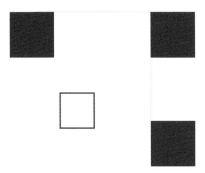

Figure 6.6

Objects that are aligned appear to be related.

Figure 6.7

Objects indented beneath other objects will appear subordinate.

Typography

Typography is an important choice in any visual interface, providing not only a platform for usable, readable, and clear labels and text, but also personality.

Typefaces

Typefaces, commonly called fonts, are generally categorized into two groups: *serif* and *sans-serif.* Serif typefaces, such as Times and Garamond, have details—serifs—on the end of the strokes that make up their letter-forms (**Figure 6.8**). Serif typefaces are easy to read and are excellent for long passages of text, as in books. Sans serif typefaces, such as Helvetica and Arial, have no or less prominent details at the ends of the strokes that make up their letterforms. They are traditionally used for shorter passages of text and for text that is meant to be scanned quickly, such as signage. Thus, sans serif typefaces have become the default choice for interaction designers in screen or physical designs. They are excellent for button labels, instructional text, and menus. Some typefaces, such as Verdana and Georgia, have been specifically designed for the screen. If you need each letter to be the same width, look for monospace or fixed-width typefaces such as Courier. For most projects, however, a typeface of medium width is best.

Times
The quick brown fox jumped over the lazy dog.

Garamond
The quick brown fox jumped over the lazy dog.

Helvetica
The quick brown fox jumped over the lazy dog.

Arial
The quick brown fox jumped over the lazy dog.

Verdana
The quick brown fox jumped over the lazy dog.

Georgia
The quick brown fox jumped over the lazy dog.

Courier
The quick brown fox jumped over the lazy dog.

Meta
The quick brown fox jumped over the lazy dog.

Univers
The quick brown fox jumped over the lazy dog.

Frutiger
The quick brown fox jumped over the lazy dog.

Figure 6.8

A collection of standard and classic typefaces.

There are a lot of typefaces out there. Avoid typefaces that appear very heavy or very light. For optimum legibility, designers can seldom go wrong choosing classic, time-tested typefaces such as Meta, Univers, and Frutiger. Avoid using lots of typefaces at once, and avoid combining typefaces that are too similar—the result will look like a mistake.

Typographic Guidelines

In general, designers should avoid using too many different type sizes and weights (book, semibold, bold, italic, black) at the same time. It's best to start with book weight and a standard point size and sparingly use other sizes and weights for things like labels and headers.

Setting text in all capital letters severely retards readability. Use uppercase and lowercase letters for optimum readability, except for single words or phrases, and never combine small caps and regular caps.

Always maintain the integrity of the typeface. Avoid stretching or distorting typefaces or putting text on a curve.

Here are some other general typographic guidelines:

▶ **Size.** Type sizes for screens are generally 9 to 12 points, unless the screen is on a mobile device, in which case sizes of 6 to 10 points are typical. Anything below 6 points is extremely difficult to read. Type sizes on physical devices (for example, on the keys of a keyboard) depend on the size of the device, but text of 6 to 9 points is fairly common.

▶ **Alignment.** Flush left and ragged right alignment is more legible than flush right or justified. Justify only text that has a long line length, and use flush right sparingly and never for long passages of text.

▶ **Rivers.** Rivers are formed when the white spaces between words seemingly line up and form a "river." Avoid these.

▶ **Widows and orphans.** Avoid widows (a word left on a line by itself) and orphans (a single word at the beginning of a column or page).

▶ **Line length.** Apply the Goldilocks Principle to the line length for blocks of text: not too long, not too short, but just right. Forty characters (about an alphabet and a half's worth of letters, spaces, and punctuation) should be about the minimum for a block of text. In general, strive for line lengths of 55 to 75 characters.

▶ **Leading.** Leading, the vertical space between lines, should be 20 percent more than the font size, typically +2 points. For example, a 10-point font should have 12-point leading, and an 11-point font should have 13-point leading. One exception to this rule is very small type (below 8 points), which needs more leading to make it more legible. *Optical gray* refers to how dense type appears; the less optical gray text is, the more readable it is. More leading makes text less optical gray. Also, the longer the line length, the more leading is required, so add leading of 3 or 4 points to long lines. The same also holds true for short line lengths, where adding leading of 2.5, 3, or 4 points is a good idea. (Never add more than 4 points, though.)

▶   **Kerning.** Kerning is the horizontal space between letters. Ideally, the spaces between the letters of a word will *appear* to be (though not necessarily *be*) even. Unless you are working in a point size larger than 18, you likely won't have to do much kerning, except possibly to tighten up a word to fit in a space. Kerning over a number of letters or words is called *tracking*. Try not to add spaces between lowercase letters. The person who would do so is the type of person who would also, in the famous words of typographer Frederic Goudy, "steal sheep."

Color

Color has a number of functions in visual interface design. While color can be used to create personality and tone, interaction designers are most interested in how color can provide cues for use. Red buttons, for instance, as on a mobile phone, can signal stop or end, while green ones can signal go or send. Color also can establish relationships between disparate objects; for example, buttons at a Web site, no matter where they are placed, could all be one color. Color can indicate importance: a highly saturated blue box will attract the eye more quickly than a pale yellow one.

However, color can be greatly misused. Most of us have seen applications or Web sites that either are flat and dull from lack of color or look like a circus from too many colors or colors that are too saturated. Designers should also remember that about 10 percent of the male population have some sort of color blindness, which renders greens and reds as shades of gray.

Color Basics

All colors have three main properties: hue, value (or brightness), and intensity (or saturation). Hue refers to the color itself, or, technically, the particular color within the optical (visible) spectrum of light. Value refers to the amount of black in a color—how dark or light it is. Intensity refers to the brightness or dullness of the color.

Designers should become familiar with the color wheel (**Figure 6.9**), which is helpful not only for choosing a color scheme, but also for avoiding color-related problems. There are three *primary colors*: red, blue, and yellow. Mixing two primary colors together creates the *secondary colors*: purple, green, and orange. *Analogous colors* are those that are adjacent to each other on the color wheel. Analogous colors are excellent for creating color schemes—try using three or four of them together, such as red, orange, and yellow, or blue, green, and yellow. *Complementary colors* are those that are across the color wheel from each other—for example, red and green. Although they have been used by artists for centuries, care should be taken when using complementary colors together. Although they will make each other vivid, used together they can also be difficult to focus on.

Figure 6.9

The color wheel. Knowing its basic principles will help designers avoid clashing colors.

The painter Josef Albers noted that a color doesn't exist until it meets another color. Designers should look at the edges of colors and see how they work together. White backgrounds tend to darken, and can even deaden, colors. Black backgrounds tend to lighten colors. Try backgrounds that aren't pure white or black, such as light gray. Very pale yellow backgrounds with black type are good for older eyes.

Care should be taken to avoid an effect called *chromostereopsis*, which occurs when two colors side by side seem to cause both colors to vibrate. Red and blue together—for instance, blue text on a red background (**Figure 6.10**)—will often create this effect, irritating viewers' eyes. In general, colored text on a colored background is difficult to execute well.

Figure 6.10

Blue text on a red
background creates
chromostereopsis.
Avoid this.

When working in color, ensure that sufficient contrast exists between the foreground color and its background. Vary the saturation and brightness to make foreground items stand out. But when initially picking a suite of colors, try to keep them all at around the same value. Colors with equal values and saturation will create a coherent, even appearance.

Since the human eye is very attuned to color and the human brain responds to color both consciously and unconsciously, color is one of the most powerful tools in visual interface design.

Material and Shape

Visual interface design isn't only about screens. What surrounds those screens—if there even is a screen—matters greatly as well. As noted in Chapter 3, the physical form of a device tells a lot about how and where the device is meant to be used. That physical form is made of some sort of material, often metal and plastic, but also wood, clay, ceramic, cloth, rubber, glass, leather, or some combination.

Each of these materials has its own characteristics, feeling different in the hand and with a different visual impact. And these basic materials themselves can have drastically different looks and feels—metal may be industrial iron or high-end brushed nickel; plastic may be a thick slab or a brittle strip. Materials also determine weight, which is an important factor especially in mobile or portable devices.

Imitating another material (typically with plastic materials) can cause a device to be viewed and treated differently. Clear plastic, although it can be firm and solid, is often treated like glass, for instance. You don't see many clear mobile phones, although they could be made.

Luke Wroblewski on Visual Interaction Design

Luke Wroblewski is an interface designer, strategist, and author of the book Site-Seeing: A Visual Approach to Web Usability *as well as numerous articles on software interface design. He sits on the board of directors of the Interaction Design Association and is a frequent presenter on topics related to interface design.*

How can visual design support (or detract) from interaction design?

In most applications, audio cues need to be used sparingly and instructional text is rarely read. As a result, the visual design bears the responsibility of communicating the possibilities, limitations, and state of interactions. It tells users what they are seeing, how it works, and why they should care.

When visual elements are applied without an understanding of the underlying interactions they are meant to support, however, the wrong message may be sent to users. Visual styling that obscures or clouds crucial interaction options, barriers, or status messages can have a significantly negative impact on user experience.

Think of visual design as the "voice" of interaction design and information architecture. It communicates the importance of (and relationships between) the content and actions within an application.

What do interaction designers need to know about visual design?

Visual design can be thought of as two interwoven parts: visual organization and personality. Visual organization utilizes the principles of perception (how we make sense of what we see) to construct a visual narrative. Through applications of contrast, visual designers can communicate the steps required to complete a task, the relationships between information, or the hierarchy between interface elements. So clearly visual organization is a key component for successful interface designs.

Unfortunately, the bulk of discussions about the effectiveness of visual design don't focus on visual organization systems. Instead, they are limited to a subjective analysis of the personality (look and feel) of an interface. Personality is achieved through a judicious selection of colors, fonts, patterns, images, and visual elements designed to communicate a particular message to an audience. But just about everyone has a color or font preference, so when asked to evaluate visual design, that's where they turn first.

Luke Wroblewski on Visual Interaction Design *Continued*

My advice to interaction designers is to take the time to learn the principles underlying visual organization. You'll be better able to communicate with the visual designers on your team and, more importantly, with the end users of your product.

What are some of the common interface mistakes that new interaction designers make?

The most common interface design mistakes I see are overstatements of visual contrast. For example, designers will want to make sure everything on a screen can be found and therefore apply an equal amount of visual weight to each element to ensure it's "discoverable." The problem is when every element on a screen is shouting to get noticed, no one gets heard. As a user, you can recognize these types of designs because your eyes bounce from one element to the next. There is no hierarchy and as a result no flow through the content and actions on the screen.

Similarly, many designers will overemphasize the differences between individual interface elements through multiple visual relationships: different font, size, color, and alignment. You don't need excess visual contrast to distinguish objects or make things findable. Think about ways to "eliminate the unnecessary so that the necessary may speak."

You talk a lot about personality. How do you provide a visual personality to your designs?

Whether you've thought about it or not, people will ascribe a personality to your product based on the way it looks and acts. Therefore, it is in your best interests to be aware of the personality you are creating for your site through visual design (or lack of it) and make certain it is telling the story you want.

Luckily, there's a huge visual vocabulary available for establishing an appropriate personality for your application. Millions of colors, hundreds of thousands of font choices, and innumerable patterns and images are all at your disposal. The trick is settling on the right combination of these for your particular needs. Consider what you want to communicate to your audience and how; then locate visual elements that convey that message in the world around you. You'll be surprised at what you can find when you look!

The material and form of any physical controls (discussed later in this chapter) are crucial components of any device. After all, if a device cannot be turned on, it can't be used. Keyboard keys need to be set firmly enough for many repeat pressings, but not so firmly so that they are a chore to press. Ergonomics and human factors come into play in the size and shape of controls. How small can a button be before most people can't press it? Should a dial have a ridged edge or be smooth?

The overall size and shape of a device are important visually as well. A thick black box made of plastic with knobs and dials on it probably belongs on the shelf with other multimedia equipment, while a thin sliver of the same black plastic about the size of a pack of cards probably slips into a purse or pocket. Does it have a strap? If so, it's supposed to be carried around. Are its buttons visible or hidden? Is the on/off control a switch or a button or a knob? There are literally dozens of design decisions for the physical form of a device, and each has meaning and, from a business standpoint, an associated cost. An extra nice button might add only an extra 2 cents to each unit, but 10 million devices later, those 2 cents have added up to $200,000.

Controls and Widgets

Most applications and devices that interaction designers currently design have some sort of visible controls for the user to use to manipulate the features of the product—a dial to control volume on a stereo, for example, or a slider to select a date range. Controls provide both the affordances needed to understand what the product is capable of and the power to realize that capability.

This section describes the basic controls that interaction designers use. This isn't a complete list because interaction designers occasionally find new ways of engaging with product functionality. Almost all of these controls have their own standard feedback mechanisms (a switch moves and stays in its new position, for instance) that interaction designers should consider.

Figure 6.11

A switch is the simplest of controls.

▶ **Switch.** A toggle switch (**Figure 6.11**) is a very simple control. It moves from one setting ("on") to another ("off") and stays there until changed.

▶ **Button.** Buttons (**Figure 6.12**) are the interaction designer's best friend. Once you begin to look for them, it's apparent that buttons are everywhere, all over our interfaces. In Microsoft Word alone, there are about 30 buttons visible at any given time. A mobile phone may have about 40 buttons: the number keys for dialing and a keyboard. A button is, at base, an item that is pressed or clicked to activate it. The button can stay pressed (a toggle button), requiring another press to reset it (like most on/off buttons), or it can reset itself automatically (like keys on a keyboard). Buttons can be used for a wide variety of actions: from changing modes (from writing text to drawing, say) to moving an item or a cursor via arrow keys. Buttons can take many forms, from tiny icons to physical squares on a floor that can be stepped on. Buttons, however, are good only for simple actions.

Figure 6.12

Buttons are an interaction designer's best friend.

▶ **Dial.** A dial (**Figure 6.13**) provides more control than a button, allowing the user to select a setting along a continuum (such as the amount of heat on a stove's burner) or to choose between different settings or modes (such as the mode for taking pictures and the mode for viewing them on a digital camera. Dials can move freely or simply turn from an established point to other established points on a wheel. Some dials, like those often found on clothes dryers, can be pushed in and pulled out, performing an action (such as turning on or off) that can vary based on the dial's rotation.

Figure 6.13

Use a dial when users need more control than a button provides.

▶ **Latch.** A latch (**Figure 6.14**) opens an otherwise tightly closed area. Latches are useful for keeping some areas or items hidden or safe until needed. They are good to use when a button or drop-down menu might be too easy to click or open. For example, latches are frequently used on handheld devices to keep the battery compartment safe.

Figure 6.14

Latches protect areas that shouldn't be accessed too frequently or easily.

▶ **Slider.** Sliders (**Figure 6.15**), like dials, are used for subtle control of a feature, often to control output such as speaker volume or the amount of data displayed, such as the number of houses on an interactive map. Sliders with more than one handle can be used to set a range within a range.

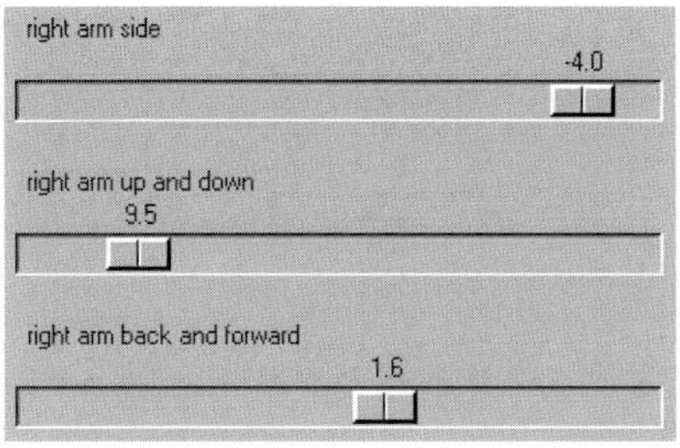

Figure 6.15

Sliders are good for subtle control. Designers seem to love sliders.

▶ **Handle.** A handle (**Figure 6.16**) is simply a protruding part of an object that allows it to be moved or, in some cases, resized. Handles on the frames of most digital windows allow the windows to be moved around the screen or resized.

Figure 6.16

Frames of digital windows act as handles.

Physical-Only Controls

Some common controls are found only in the physical world and not on screens (although they can certainly manipulate objects on a screen).

▶ **Jog dial.** A jog dial (**Figure 6.17**) is a type of dial that can be manipulated with a single finger, usually a thumb. It can be dial-like, or it can be a pad of buttons, typically used on small devices for moving a cursor or moving through menus. Jog dials are somewhat difficult to control, especially for young children and the elderly.

Figure 6.17

Jog dials are typically found on small devices such as digital cameras and mobile phones.

▶ **Joystick.** A joystick (**Figure 6.18**) is a physical device typically used in digital gaming or in other applications that require rapid movement and intensive manipulation of remote physical or digital objects. Joysticks can move in any direction or can be constrained to move only left to right or only up and down.

Figure 6.18

Joysticks allow for control of either physical or digital objects from afar.

▶ **Trackball.** A trackball (**Figure 6.19**) is a physical device for manipulating a cursor or other digital or physical objects. Trackballs are typically in a stationary base, but the ball itself moves in any direction. A computer mouse is a trackball in a case, usually with buttons.

Figure 6.19

A mouse is really just a trackball in a case.

Digital-Only Controls

While many controls are found in both the physical, analog world and the digital one, some controls are found only on screens. These digital controls have grown from the original graphical user interface (GUI) vocabulary that was invented at Xerox PARC in the 1970s, reinvented in the 1980s in the Macintosh and PC operating systems, and added to and expanded by Web conventions in the 1990s.

▶   **Check box**. A check box (**Figure 6.20**) enables users to select items from a short list.

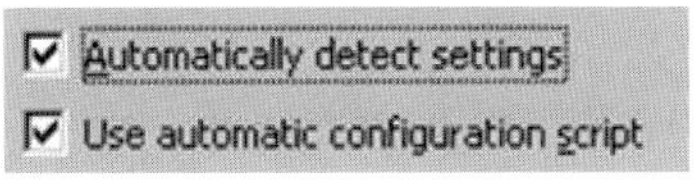

Figure 6.20

Check boxes allow users to select items from a list.

▶   **Radio button.** Radio buttons (**Figure 6.21**) enable users to choose a single item from a selection. Typically, these are used to constrain selections, when only one answer is allowed ("Do you have blond hair?" Yes/No).

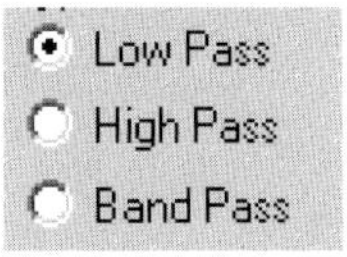

Figure 6.21

Radio buttons typically allow selection of only one item at a time.

▶   **Twist.** Twists (**Figure 6.22**) turn up or down, either revealing or hiding content or a menu in a panel.

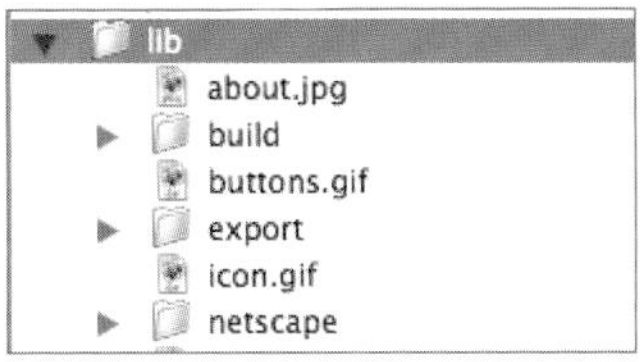

Figure 6.22

A twist is a type of latch that reveals or hides items, such as the contents of a folder.

▶   **Scroll bar.** Scroll bars (**Figure 6.23**) enable users to move content within a particular window or panel. Scroll bars can be vertical or horizontal. Scroll bars themselves can be manipulated via the cursor or buttons (for instance, by using arrow keys).

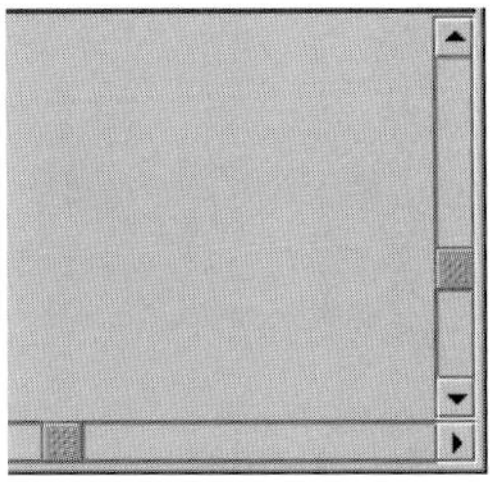

Figure 6.23

Vertical scroll bars are common, but horizontal scroll bars, because they are more difficult to manipulate, have never caught on.

▶ **Drop-down menu.** Drop-down menus (**Figure 6.24**) allow designers to cluster navigation, functionality, or content together without having to display it all at once. Drop-down menus can be displayed by rolling over them, or they can be opened with a click. They can retract after a selection has been made or the cursor rolls off them, though not necessarily.

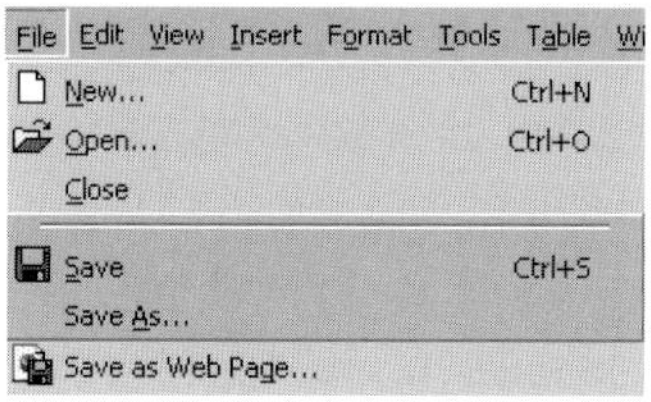

Figure 6.24

Drop-down menus have many variations.

▶ **Multiple-selection list (or list box).** Multiple-selection lists (**Figure 6.25**) enable users to select multiple items in a list.

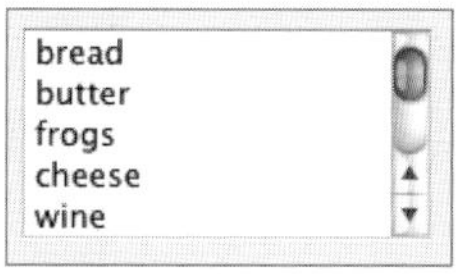

Figure 6.25

A multiple-selection list allows users to select multiple items in long lists.

▶ **Text box.** Text boxes (**Figure 6.26**) enable users to enter numbers, letters, or symbols. They can be as small as (and constrained to) a single character or as large as the whole screen.

Figure 6.26

Text boxes are the primary vehicle for (relatively) free input.

▶ **Spin box.** Spin boxes (**Figure 6.27**) are text boxes with additional controls that enable users to manipulate what is inside the text box without having to type a value. They are good for suggesting values in what otherwise might be an ambiguous text box.

Figure 6.27

Spin boxes combine text boxes with small buttons.

The combination of one (and usually more) controls plus the system response is called a *widget*. Widgets are the building blocks of any application or device. An MP3 player, for instance, is made of widgets: one for controlling volume, one for controlling the playing of music files, one for organizing files, one for exporting files, and so on. In each case, the user uses controls to perform an action, and the system responds. All applications and devices are made up of widgets.

Icons

Many digital products use icons. Icons are visual metaphors representing features or actions. They act as both shortcuts and visual reminders ("Oh that's right, I can print this!") for features for users.

The choice of visual metaphor is crucial, however. A confusing image can obscure much more than it can illuminate. For example, the disk icon (**Figure 6.28**) has come to mean "save," even though, increasingly, many young people have never seen a floppy disk (except perhaps this icon!). Then again, it is difficult to imagine what image could replace it.

Figure 6.28

The visual of a floppy disk no longer makes sense for the Save icon.

Perhaps for this reason, plus the influence of Web style on interfaces, icons have fallen out of favor in recent years, replaced by just text. Using text can, of course, be a problem in languages other than English. For example, German words can be notoriously long and may have trouble fitting in the space required. Icons are still found in feature-rich applications with tool bars, such as Adobe Photoshop and Microsoft Word, as it is often impractical, if not impossible, to fit all the frequently used features on the screen otherwise.

One exception to this trend is mobile devices. With screen and physical real estate being extremely limited, icons for indicators such as signal and battery strength are essential. Words would simply take up too much space.

Case Study: Gmail with Google Talk

The Company

Google, the search engine colossus.

The Problem

In some ways, the division between e-mail and instant messaging is a false one. They are both communication tools, albeit for different situations. Sometimes users need a quick message, and sometimes a longer one. Real-time online discussion can be more appropriate than an e-mail message, and vice versa. However, users typically have to use two separate applications for doing these two tasks.

The Process

Google decided to create one centralized place where users could send both e-mail and instant messages, depending on the situation. The company already had both an e-mail application (Gmail) and an instant messenger (Google Talk). Deciding on what useful integration between two communication systems really meant was the underlying challenge. After defining some basic performance metrics—the application had to be as responsive as a desktop application—the engineers built a proof-of-concept technology demo. Meanwhile, the designers created sketches and mockups focused on a window management system that made multitasking using inboxes, e-mails, and instant message chat windows possible.

A prototype of one possible direction (not taken) for the integration of the two programs.

Case Study: Gmail with Google Talk *Continued*

The Solution

The left pane of the Gmail interface was widened slightly to accommodate a buddy list. Logging onto Gmail automatically makes a user's online presence visible to potential chat partners, and a drop-down widget for changing availability (including signing out of chat) remembers the user's most recent state across sessions so that those uninterested in chatting aren't forced into it. The chat experience was changed from a more modal interaction in the demo to one with a less obtrusive location that allows concurrent navigation within e-mails while chats are open. The notification system for new chat messages includes high-contrast changes in color and an optional audible plink. Like e-mails, chats are archived to be easily searchable. Emoticons appear sideways looking just like the text characters that trigger them, but then, in keeping with Google's sometimes quirky style, they rotate and animate their way to facial expressions.

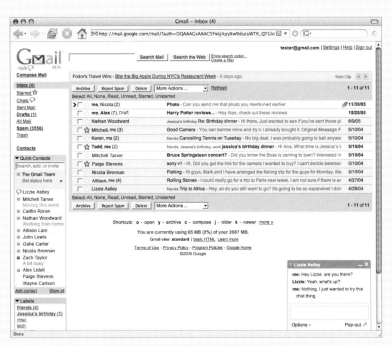

The launched product: Google Talk is integrated into Gmail.

Sound

Sound, as pointed out in Chapter 3, is both over- and underused in interaction design. Nearly everyone has had the experience of going to a Web site only to have it suddenly blast music, sending you scrambling to turn the thing off. But sound, done well, can subtly enhance an interface.

Sounds can be ambient cues that something has happened so that users don't have to constantly visually monitor the application for changes. This use of sound is especially helpful in applications with frequent changes that may occur while the user is otherwise occupied. A ding! indicates that an e-mail has arrived. The door-opening sound indicates that a buddy has signed onto the instant messenger client. The ring of a mobile phone indicates that a text message has arrived. These are all helpful sound cues.

How can you tell if a sound will, over time, become an annoyance? Record it. Test it on others and see what they think. Listen to it frequently. Use the application yourself and see if you become annoyed at it. If you do, probably others will as well.

Standards

There is a perennial debate among interaction designers about how closely to follow interface standards and when to break them. Do all applications have to work in a similar way? Should Ctrl-C or Command-C always copy whatever is selected? Does every menu bar have to have the same headings (File, Edit, View, and so on)? Both Microsoft and Apple have standards guidelines that can be downloaded online and are religiously followed by many. Usability gurus such as Jakob Nielsen promote and swear by them.

There are certainly good reasons for having and using standards. Over many years, designers have trained users to expect certain items to be located in certain places (the company logo goes at the top left of a Web site) and certain features to work in a particular way (pressing Ctrl-Z undoes the last command). A design that ignores these standards means that your users will have to learn something different, something that doesn't work like all their other applications work. A deviation from the standard can cause frustration and annoyance.

So why ever violate or alter standards?

For my money, interaction design guru Alan Cooper solved this dilemma with his axiom: *Obey standards unless there is a truly superior alternative.* That is, ignore standards only when a new layout or feature is markedly, significantly better than what the users have previously used. Feel free to propose a new method of cutting and pasting, but it had better be unequivocally better than what users are accustomed to now, creating a new standard. New standards don't have to be radical departures from the old standards, but even a slight change to them should be made with care.

Interfaces Without Faces

We are arriving at a time when screens aren't the only—and possibly not even the primary—way we interact with the digital world or the way the digital world reacts to us. With the dawn of ubiquitous computing environments (see Chapter 9) in the near future, people will need to engage with many different sorts of objects that have microprocessors and sensors built into them, from rooms to appliances to bicycles.

As novelist William Gibson famously reminds us, the future is here; it's just unevenly distributed. There are already examples of these faceless interfaces, such as the dreaded voice-operated phone systems that now dominate customer service. Your car, too, may have a faceless interface, letting out a screech when you accidentally leave the headlights on.

The controls for these faceless interfaces are the human body: our voices, our movements, and simply our presence.

Voice

Voice-controlled interfaces are already with us, particularly on phones. People can call their banks and perform transactions or dial their mobile phones with just their voices. Voice commands typically control limited functionality, and the device typically has to be ready to receive voice commands, either because it functions only via voice commands (as with automated phone systems and some voice-controlled devices—see **Figure 6.29**), or because it has been prepared to receive voice commands, as with mobile phones that allow voice dialing. What are difficult to create, from both technical and design perspectives, are voice-controlled interfaces in public spaces, when a device or system is always listening for a command to do something. How will the system know that someone is issuing it a command? Will it be like old *Star Trek* episodes where the crew actually addresses the computer? "Computer, get me all the files relating to geeks." As with other body-based controls discussed in this section, this is a design challenge that has yet to be solved.

Figure 6.29

The author screams at Blendie, a voice-controlled blender by Kellie Dobson, to get it to frappe.

Gestures

There is a scene in the sci-fi movie *Minority Report* in which Tom Cruise stands before a semitransparent screen and simply by gesturing with his hands he moves things around the screen, zooming documents and video in and out. This scene has become a touchstone for gesture-based controls.

To most computers and devices, people consist of two things: hands and eyes. The rest of the human body is ignored. But as our devices gain more awareness of the movement of the human body through Global Positioning System (GPS) sensors and sudden-motion sensors (SMSs), for instance, they will become better able to respond to the complete human body, including to gestures. Indeed, some mobile phones are coming equipped with tilt motion sensors, so that users can, for example, "pour" data from their phone into another device.

Determining what gestures (like pouring) are appropriate for initiating actions on what devices and in what environments is a task for interaction designers in the next decade.

Presence

Some systems respond simply to a person's presence. Many interactive games and installations, such as Danny Rozin's "Wooden Mirror" (**Figure 6.30**), respond to a body's being near their sensors. With sensors and cameras being built into laptops such as Apple's MacBook, we'll certainly see more applications that respond to presence, when users are active in front of their computers.

Figure 6.30

The "Wooden Mirror" creates the image of what is in front of it by flipping wooden blocks within its frame.

There are many design decisions to be made with presence-activated systems. Consider a room with sensors and environmental controls, for example. Does the system respond immediately when someone enters the room, turning on lights and climate-control systems, or does it pause for a few moments, in case someone was just passing through?

In addition, sometimes users may not want their presence known. Users may not want their activities and location known for any number of reasons, including personal safety and simple privacy. Designers will have to determine how and when a user can become "invisible" to presence-activated systems.

Summary

Interface design isn't only about making a device or application look attractive. It's about finding the appropriate representation—visual, audible, physical—that inspires user input and guides system output. It's about embodying the characteristics of good interaction design as expressed in Chapter 3. It's about finding the right affordances so that users know what a device can do and how to make the device do it. And it's about making an appropriately pleasing application or device that people find useful and usable and want to integrate into their lives.

7

Smart Applications and Clever Devices

Interaction designers are used to focusing on the task at hand, what users want to do *at that moment*—perhaps focusing too much. This has led to the creation of digital tools for small, discrete tasks (sell a stock, crop a photo, send an e-mail message, send a text message). While these tools are very useful, they are not so helpful for designing for the long view: designing for what happens over time.

When interaction designers step back from the task at hand, it's obvious that the devices and applications we currently design and use are, for the most part, dumb. They don't know where they are; they have no context. They don't know who we are. They don't know how we engage with them or what we use them for. They can't remember what we did with them a few minutes ago, much less yesterday or over the sometimes years that we use them. They are dumb.

This needs to change.

As our world grows ever more complex, our tools need to manage more of that complexity. We need smart applications and clever devices.

Designing for Multitasking

For the past two decades, interaction designers have been designing the equivalent of digital hammers—really nice hammers—that do the task at hand (hammering digital nails) but not much else. Our digital tools mostly perform single tasks when they could be *multitasking*: collecting data about how they are being used and by whom, subtly adjusting themselves to become more personal and more useful.

For humans, multitasking can reduce the quality and quantity of work, but computers mostly don't have this limitation. Most of the time, our computers, mobile phones, and digital appliances sit idle, waiting for a command. Most processing time between keystrokes and cursor movements passes unused. Our computers, mobile phones, and electronic devices are ridiculously powerful now, thanks to the fulfillment of Moore's Law (see Chapter 3), and are starting to contain more memory space than most of us are likely to use. Why shouldn't our devices use this spare memory and power to gather data about our behavior and optimize themselves based on that?

Thanks to increased processing speed and memory, computers and other digital devices can register and record our behaviors like nothing else—except perhaps royal manservants and private detectives—has ever done. And yet, for the most part, devices either don't capture this information or don't use it well. Sure, the occasional site welcomes users back, and your mobile phone remembers whom you last called, but these behaviors are pretty rudimentary.

Most digital devices and applications have no sense of history, but history is information that can be gathered and acted upon. If every time you visit a Web site you go to the same page, chances are good that when you visit that site again you'll want to go to that page—and the site or the browser should somehow acknowledge that, either by simply taking you there or in some way making it easy for you to get there. In 2002, the BBC's online site, BBCi, was redesigned to accomplish just that (**Figure 7.1**). As a user makes repeated trips to the site, a path is worn through the home page. Sections the user visits frequently slowly become visually distinct via a darker shade of color. Thus, it is easy for return users to find the sections they visit frequently. The site collects data about a user's behavior and then adjusts the site to make it more useful for that user. BBCi called its redesign The Glass Wall.

Figure 7.1

BBCi redesigned its site so that users wear personal paths through it. The left screen shows the original palette, the middle screen shows the screen after several visits, and the right screen shows the palette of a frequent user.

Amazon understood this in 1996 and, despite its current cluttered pages, still gets some things right, such as showing users where they've been recently (**Figure 7.2**). Amazon famously, of course, goes one step further, comparing individual user's data to the huge pool of data collected from all Amazon users, showing the "People who bought this also bought…" plus the really interesting "What do customers ultimately buy after viewing items like this?" items. Amazon, naturally, has a motive for doing this, but this additional information, this added value for the users that the users did nothing to obtain except perform their usual shopping tasks, is one reason why Amazon has succeeded brilliantly while so many other online retailers have gone under.

Figure 7.2

The Amazon Web site multitasks constantly, comparing your data to other users' data.

BBCi and Amazon made completing tasks *in the future* easier and more interesting for users, and that's something worth designing. Note, too, that users don't have to set preferences or tell either of these sites what they are interested in doing. The sites learn this from behaviors their users *are already engaged in*. The onus isn't on users to customize their experiences; the sites themselves are smart enough to do it. They multitask.

Another important point about these sites is that the changes are *subtle* and *appropriate*—the sites multitask and adjust in ways that users appreciate. Microsoft's infamous Clippy ("It looks like you are writing a letter!") is an example of unsubtle multitasking. Although the feature was meant to be helpful, it quickly (read *instantly*) became annoying and intrusive. Yes, I'm writing a letter, but I can format my own letters, thanks. This "help" isn't appropriate because typing a letter isn't a difficult task that most users have trouble doing on their own. Clippy's "help" isn't helpful at all; it's intrusive and demeaning. Which brings us to another key point: multitasking should be appropriate, meaning that it should help users do the things they could never do on their own, or things that would otherwise be tedious to do on their own. Individual users would have no way of knowing what other users bought unless Amazon told them. Similarly, users could keep track of the various sections they visit at BBCi, but it is much easier and certainly much less tedious to let the site do it.

Here is another example of the use of the history of a user's behavior. I frequently misspell the word *ubiquitous*, always adding in an extra *i* at the end: "ubiquitious." There's no reason why, after one correction of this word using the spell checker, I should ever have to spell check this word again. The application should record this data ("My user misspells *ubiquitous*") and auto-correct it the next time I misspell it. After all, how many words could I really be spelling? And since my word processor runs on a computer that is connected to the Internet almost 24/7, there's no reason why this little bit of data couldn't be shared among other users of this application, so that if other people misspell *ubiquitous* with an extra *i*, the application can correct them as well.

Note   *Obviously, when collecting information based on user history, privacy issues arise: what data is being shared and how easily can that data be traced back to individual users? Suppose, for instance, I am frequently misspelling the word* diarrhea. *Would I want that shared? Or traced back to me? And just what kind of documents am I writing here anyway? Designers of applications and devices that multitask must be hyper-aware of what data users may not want collected or shared, and users should always be able to opt out of the collecting or sharing of any personal information.*

Now imagine tools that can self-correct based on data about how they are being used. Suppose that users are having trouble clicking a button to submit a form. If an application is aware enough to notice where, when, and how clicks are being made, it can move the button or increase its sensitivity for the individual user, and even potentially for all users, if the application notices the same behaviors happening frequently enough.

Of course, data doesn't have to come in only through a user. Devices and applications designed for multitasking can collect information about not only how, but also where and when they are being used—context and environment also can be inputs to applications and devices. This information can then be used to improve the product. Why, when I turn it on at night, doesn't my iPod automatically turn on its backlight? It has a clock built into it, so it should (or could) be aware of the time. I'm likely to need the backlight at night, and when I don't, I can always turn it off.

Likewise, why doesn't my e-mail client adjust itself to check for e-mail more frequently during working hours than on weekends? Again, it has a clock and calendar built into it, so why not leverage those? There is no reason that, when my laptop is idle, my e-mail program couldn't analyze my usage patterns and adapt to me.

There is also no reason that devices and objects can't perform complementary tasks at the same time. For example, my car, while taking me from place to place, could also be sensing and reporting the traffic conditions. Factors such as the speed of the car could be used to determine whether traffic is flowing smoothly, and that information could be shared with car navigation systems and maps such as Yahoo's traffic map (**Figure 7.3**).

Figure 7.3

Imagine how much better Yahoo's traffic map would be if the data was an amalgamation of information coming from cars on the road.

Instant-messaging clients perform complementary tasks well with their inclusion of status messages in their buddy lists (**Figure 7.4**). Rather than simply showing that a user is online, idle, or away, status messages turn the buddy list into another means of communication. For many, especially teens and young adults, the status message is now as important as the instant messages!

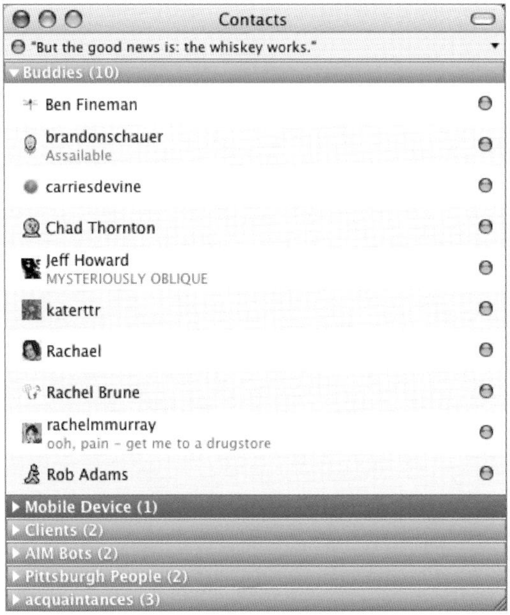

Figure 7.4

Adium's buddy list. Status messages take what could be just a simple conveyance of information and turn it into a whole new channel of communication.

Designing for Connection

What we've just been discussing under the guise of multitasking is *adaptation*: changes in the form, content, and functionality of devices and applications based on how and where they are used. With adaptation, users feel more emotional attachment—a connection—to their tools.

People use three primary ways to make devices and applications their own: customization and personalization, adaptation, and hacking. Collectively, these approaches facilitate a tighter bond between users and their tools.

Customization and Personalization

Figure 7.5

A customized mobile phone, encrusted with rhinestones. It's common in Asia to customize devices in this way, often with real jewels.

Customization and personalization are commonly used interchangeably, but in interaction design, they have specific, different meanings. Customization occurs when users alter the appearance of an object or application, either through the application of appearance-changing products (from sequins to spray paint to stickers) on physical objects (**Figure 7.5**) or, on digital products, through the use of controls (this is sometimes called skinning). There are whole industries, especially in the automotive field, built around customization. Although customization can make something look very different, it changes an object in a very limited way. It modifies only the surface of an object.

Personalization is a step beyond customization. Personalization alters the functionality of an entity to better reflect individual choices. It changes not only the surface. Personalizing changes how something *works*. Changing a shortcut keystroke—for instance, replacing Command-X, the Cut command on a Mac, with Command–K—is an example of personalization.

Personalization requires the object, if it isn't wholly digital, to have some sort of digital component that the user can use to indicate preferences and settings. Personalization requires users to explicitly set preferences (**Figure 7.6**) for the variables that can be personalized (how often to check e-mail, default sound volume, speed-dial numbers, and so on).

Figure 7.6

The Preferences window in Microsoft Word. To set preferences, you have to stop what you're doing, find the preference you want, and set it. If you had to do this frequently, the process would be disruptive.

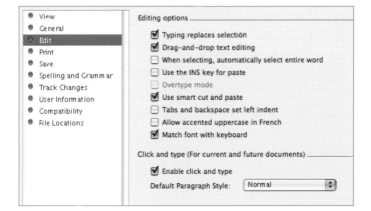

Adaptation

The alternative to deliberate manipulation and maintenance is adaptation. Adaptive tools change their form, content, and features based on how and where they are used.

The present world is full of static objects that force people to adapt to them, either by customizing or personalizing (or by hacking, discussed later in the chapter) or simply making do. But by harnessing the increased power of digital devices, interaction designers can create objects that learn, react, respond, understand context, and perform tasks that have personal meaning. These smart, clever devices and applications respond to people by changing shape—their form and content—depending on the context of use.

Adaptation is an ongoing process that unfolds over long time periods. Thus, it takes into account life changes that traditional products are not equipped to respond to or understand. Suppose, for example, I go on safari and can't check e-mail for several weeks. With my current e-mail client, if I don't specifically give it instructions (for instance, by setting the Out of Office option), my e-mail will simply pile up. An adaptive e-mail client, however, would notice my sudden drop-off in checking and clearing out mail by comparing my usage to my usual activity. The application would conclude (rightly) that something was different and adjust accordingly. It might, for instance, eventually contact e-mail senders in my address book and let them know that I haven't yet read their e-mail.

Adaptation can, of course, get really annoying if it isn't done well. Changes made too swiftly or too radically can be disruptive. Maybe you are doing something on a whim, like buying a Jessica Simpson single. You don't necessarily want your iTunes account to suddenly start purchasing all of Ms. Simpson's oeuvre for you.

Ideally, changes made by adaptive products should be small and should build over time. And if the system guesses wrong about a user's behavior, there needs to be a means of letting the system know that it guessed wrong.

Several years ago, *The New York Times* reported that many TiVo users who watched any TV show with a homosexual theme or character suddenly found that every show TiVo suggested to them had homosexual themes and characters. If this wasn't what a user wanted, the only way to make a change was to reset the whole TiVo device. Users need to be able to make corrections to a system's assumptions. And, as with multitasking, adaptation needs to be subtle and appropriate.

Achieving Flow

Another important concept to keep in mind when designing adaptation is that it isn't only the application or device that's adapting. There is a back and forth between the product and the user; they adapt and respond to each other.

Suppose, for example, that a user is learning an adaptive drawing application. At first, the user is crude and the system is simple. But as the user grows in skill and becomes more comfortable with the program, the program slowly becomes more sophisticated, allowing more complex methods. As the program becomes more challenging, the user has to learn more sophisticated techniques. If the user is struggling, the application may become easier to prevent frustration. The two entities react and respond to each other.

The purpose of this back and forth is to achieve what psychology professor Mihaly Csikszentmihalyi described as *flow* (**Figure 7.7**). Flow, as described by Csikszentmihalyi, is "being completely involved in an activity for its own sake. The ego falls away. Time flies. Every action, movement, and thought follows inevitably from the previous one, like playing jazz. Your whole being is involved, and you're using your skills to the utmost."

Figure 7.7

Flow diagram, based on the work of Mihaly Csikszentmihalyi. If a task is too challenging for a person's skill level, it causes anxiety. If it is too easy, it causes boredom. When skill matches challenge at a high level, this condition is called flow.

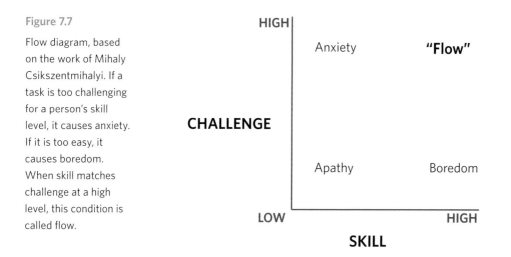

Flow, and ideally, adaptation, involve finding the correct balance between the challenge of the task and the skills of the user. Too much challenge produces anxiety; too little produces boredom. Adaptive devices and applications, if well designed, help users achieve this balance, this flow.

Designing for Adaptation

In designing for adaptation, interaction designers need to understand the deep structure of their products, but allow the surface structure to be adaptable and responsive. Designers have to determine what pieces of functionality and form are so central to the product that they never adapt. Designers also have to determine what are the "moving parts," and how those parts can change. Will the changes be digital, such as wearing a path through a Web site as with BBCi, or also physical, as with the Adidas_1, Adidas' athletic shoe that changes its physical form to conform to the way that the wearer runs? One thing designers have to wrestle with in designing adaptive products is their loss of control over the final product. (Such control is probably an illusion anyway.) Adaptive products change and grow, sometimes—probably often—in ways that the designer never expected. They have no final product, no finished form. The users co-create these products, because the products adapt to them, not to the designer's will.

Designers Shelley Evenson (see the interview in Chapter 8) and John Rheinfrank came up with a set of guidelines for creating adaptive products:

▶   **Let users do.** Make sure the activity that the user is performing is of real value. Let the user's actions and the subsequent changes in the application or device feel as though they have been designed for the user personally.

▶   **Orient.** Give users a journey they can take. Don't steer; just provide a map to help users visualize what they want to accomplish and plan where they want to go.

▶   **Let users win.** Reward users when they accomplish something.

▶   **Push.** Help users learn. Help them reveal their potential, but don't let them just get by. Combine doing with understanding. Give users a skill they can use.

▶   **Sense and respond.** Personalize the application or device for each user. Let users feel that the artifact is alive. Make its operation transparent.

▶ **Connect.** Help users make connections with the subject matter or across destinations with other people.

▶ **Immerse.** Plunge users into the experience, so that users can't tell the difference between themselves and the device, it is so much a part of them.

With a successful adaptive design, the product *fits* the user's life and environment as though it were custom made.

Hacking

The traditional approaches to interaction design (see Chapter 2) don't provide for unknown needs. They are, for the most part, good for designing products that will be used in particular ways. But interaction designers need to realize that once a product is launched, users will use it in unexpected ways and for unexpected purposes. This is what hacking is all about.

Hacking is the repurposing of a product for a task that it was never intended to perform (**Figure 7.8**). It can be as simple as using a screwdriver to open a bottle cap, or as complicated as rigging a telephone system to provide free calls.

Figure 7.8

A hack of an iPod by Collin Allen to connect it to an external hard drive.

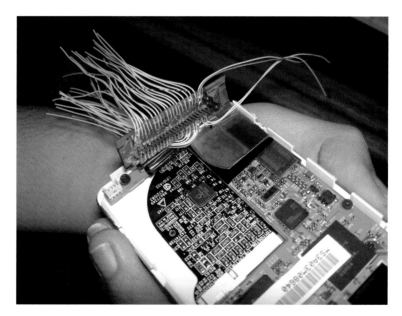

Hacking can be benign as well as destructive. Sometimes hacking involves adding functionality—for instance, adding a self-created phone book to a mobile phone. Sometimes hacking simply makes a political or social point—for instance, several years ago, in a guerilla art project, the voice chips in Barbie and G.I. Joe dolls were swapped, leaving G.I. Joe saying things like "I love shopping!" and Barbie issuing commands like "Move out, soldier!"

Hacking can be thought of as a deep expression of personalization, of forcefully adapting a product and shaping it to a person's will, whether the person "owns" the product or not. It is a way of controlling systems that otherwise the user would have no control over, such as an operating system or a government bureaucracy or even children's dolls.

Since all products (and, indeed, services) can be hacked, should interaction designers encourage hacking? And if so, how? These are unanswered questions.

One reason to encourage hacking, even unofficially, is that hacking can bring to light new uses for a product—uses that can then be officially designed for and marketed. That new feature a hacker added to your spreadsheet program may be useful to all users of the application. Those torn tennis balls that grandpa put on the feet of his walker could suggest ways in which walkers can be improved—or even whole new products (**Figure 7.9**).

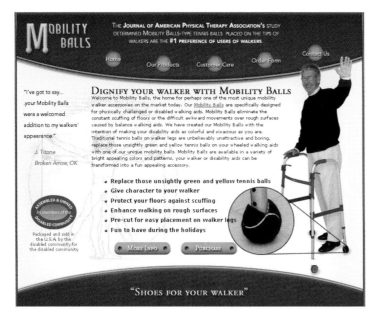

Figure 7.9

Mobility Balls used a hack (tennis balls on the feet of walkers) to make an actual product.

Obviously, no company wants destructive hacking. At the least, it can raise privacy and public relations issues. You can be certain that Mattel was unhappy about the hacking of Barbie and G.I. Joe. Some companies, particularly car companies, turn a deliberately blind eye to it, for while hacking of cars does bad things to warranties, say, it also creates demand for certain types of cars that are known to be easily hackable, such as the Honda Civic of the 1990s.

Layers

One way to design for hackability is to use *layers*—a concept first discussed by architectural theorist Stewart Brand but taken up by IBM engineer Tom Moran (**Figure 7.10**). The upper, or "fast," layers are where frequent changes take place. Lower, or "slow," layers are more stable and foundational. If products are designed so that the upper layers are more exposed (if the *seams* show, in other words), hackers can play with those, leaving the bottom layers to provide continuity and possibly to eventually integrate changes made in the upper levels.

For example, in a typical, non-Flash or Flex Web application, the top layer (typically called the presentation layer or, really, the interface) is usually composed of HTML, XML, and CSS. The next layer down is a logic layer, which contains much of the functionality, often in what is called middleware. Lower still are the layers that hold the databases, data sources, and server software. Even lower are the layers that contain the physical servers.

Figure 7.10

A diagram based on the work of Stewart Brand and Tom Moran. The top, or "fast," layers can change more rapidly, while the bottom, or "slow," layers provide stability. Changes made to the top layers can make their way down to the bottom layers over time.

Fast Layers
Can change more frequently and easily

Stuff	Post-it notes, blog posts, configuration
Services	Shipping times, prices, customer service
Skin	Mobile phone cases, look and feel

Slow Layers
Provide stability and continuity

| Structure | Operating systems, middleware, functionality |
| Site | Databases, servers, hardware |

If an application is designed so that those in the know (or those so inclined) can find the seams between some of these layers (for instance, from instructions hidden in the visible source code), then hackers can hack those locations to their heart's content. They can hack the upper layers (the CSS in particular) with the least amount of disruption—they can make the application look like anything they want. But it's unlikely that any company will want hackers tinkering with its databases and servers, so those are placed in the lower levels.

Some companies expose layers out of necessity, and some to afford hacking. Microsoft and Apple both have application program interfaces (APIs) that expose middle layers so that third-party developers can write applications on top of their operating systems. Google, in its Google Maps API, encourages the use of middle layers for the creation of maps, making it, in effect, a platform for developers, designers, and, yes, hackers to create new applications on.

Note   *An API is a set of commands, functions, and protocols that allows programmers to use predefined functions to interact with a system.*

Dan Hill on Hackability and Adaptation

Dan Hill is the head of interactive technology and design for BBC Radio and Music Interactive. He's charged with designing and building the BBC's radio and music-based interactive offerings across Web, digital TV, and mobile platforms.

Can products be made hackable, or are all products hackable?

Effectively, all products are hackable. If we define a hackable product as "a product capable of being modified by its user," then we've seen pretty much everything hacked.

But if this definition appears too wide to be useful, it's worth noting the range of products that have been hacked, apparently irrespective of size, solidity, complexity. Cars have been hacked—witness the ever-vibrant custom-car movement; buildings are endlessly modified and customized from day one; clothes often are; musical instruments often are; even apparently perfectly "finished" modernist products like Dieter Rams's Braun hi-fis have been heavily modified. Likewise the iPod, despite its hermetically sealed appearance.

Dan Hill on Hackability and Adaptation *Continued*

What can be designed into products to make them more hackable?

For me, this indicates a reversal of some traditional design thinking. The maxim that "when design is working properly, you don't notice it" (this last from Germaine Greer, no less) is less useful with hackability in mind. If we are to invite the user in, we need to leave some of the seams and traces open for others to explore, some sense of what the process of design, or un-design, might entail. Naoto Fukasawa's idea that "good design means not leaving traces of the designer" makes sense in terms of reinforcing humility in the designer, but leaving traces of the design itself may be very useful to users.

Matthew Chalmers suggests we indicate a product's "seams" so that it might convey how it can be appropriated or adapted. This is beyond affordances (which concern predefined usage). This sense that the fabric of the product should communicate its constituent parts and how they are assembled runs counter to "invisible computing" thinking and much user-centered design, which argues that interfaces should get out of the way. Yet Chalmers' notion of "seamful systems (with beautiful seams)" is powerful when seen in the context of enabling hackability.

Creation of hackable products could include the following techniques:

▶   Make sure affordances and seams are clear and malleable.

▶   Enable interrogation, cloning, and manipulation on particular layers.

▶   Learn from the malleability, object-oriented nature, and social behavior of code.

▶   Build products that are self-aware in terms of behavior/usage, which then present those findings back to users.

▶   Enable products to emerge from this behavior, as well as from design research.

▶   Enable social interaction around products.

What are the qualities of adaptive designs?

The language around hackability is often littered with "hooks," "sockets," "plugs," "handles," and so on. With adaptive design, drawing from the language of architecture more than code, we have a more graceful, refined vocabulary of "enabling change in fast layers," "building on stability in slow layers," "designing space to evolve," "time being the best designer," and so on. This suggests that there could be a distinction, that adaptive design is perhaps the process designed to enable careful articulation and evolution, as opposed to hackability's more open-ended nature.

Dan Hill on Hackability and Adaptation *Continued*

However, they still draw from the same basic concepts: of design being an ongoing social process between designer and user; of products evolving over time; of enabling the system to learn across an architecture of loosely coupled layers; of not overdesigning.

In adaptive design, designers must enable the experience/object to "learn," and users to be able to "teach" the experience/object. So it's a two-way interaction, in which the user wants to adapt the product, to make it useful to him or her. Therefore, the designers must concentrate on enabling this adaptation in order to achieve a useful experience, rather than attempting to direct the experience toward usefulness themselves. Designers shouldn't aim to control, but to enable.

You've spoken on putting "creative power in the hands of nondesigners." How do interaction designers go about doing that?

First, in order to create these more adaptable products, interaction designers will need to work within multidisciplinary environments, communicating coherently with software developers and other disciplines. This means really understanding code; it doesn't necessarily mean coding, although that can be a useful communications medium.

Second, interaction designers will need to work with these nondesigners, often directly. The notion of design being an ongoing, social process means that designers have a responsibility to work with products and experiences after they've launched. This doesn't necessarily fit many of the development methodologies, and indeed business models, that interaction designers traditionally work in. But putting designers into direct contact with nondesigners will enable them to truly adapt products to their own needs, creating genuinely engaging experiences. This is a form of design literacy, perhaps, but also product literacy. It should mean being transparent in one's practice rather than obscuring the process of design.

Ambient Devices

Most of the digital devices we use now and the applications therein require a large expenditure of our time and attention. We have to monitor them, customize them, and attend to them when they beep at us, flash alerts, issue reminders to upgrade or register, or tell us when something is wrong. Many people spend an inordinate amount of time responding to their devices' demands instead of doing their work. This is where ambient devices and what computer scientists Marc Weiser and John Seely Brown named "calm technologies" come in.

Ambient devices (which are really a subset of calm technologies) don't ask for attention. They exist on the periphery of human senses, offering information, but not insisting that people pay attention or act on that information. They aren't alarms, and if they go unnoticed, that is fine. They are supposed to be unobtrusive.

Personal ambient devices (**Figure 7.11**) haven't really caught on, except as novelty items. The major potential for ambient devices may be in public places (see "The Source" case study). Imagine a parking structure where the outside of the building indicates how full it is. Or a sports stadium whose lights change based on how the home team is doing. Or a water fountain that changes its spray depending on the weather forecast. The possibilities are endless.

Figure 7.11

An umbrella that displays weather data in its handle designed by David Rose for Ambient Devices. If the chance of rain is 100 percent, the light pulses 100 times a minute. If rain is less likely, the pulsing decreases proportionately.

Case Study: The Source

The Company

Greyworld, a group of London-based artists and designers, commissioned by The London Stock Exchange.

The Problem

Greyworld wanted an engaging, visual representation of what for most people is a confusing tangle of data: the stock market.

The Process

Greyworld took six months to build what was eventually called The Source, an eight-story-high sculpture installed in the atrium of the new London Stock Exchange building. The Source is made up of 729 spheres with LEDs inside them that are suspended from cables that stretch to the top of the building. Each sphere can move independently up and down its cable, allowing the spheres to form shapes and patterns. Their internal lights can form other fleeting shapes.

The Source consists of 729 spheres and took six months to build. Here the spheres move into a pattern suggested by the state of the market.

Case Study: The Source *Continued*

The Solution

The Source is manipulated by a computer running Python scripts that fluidly moves the spheres into dynamic shapes that reflect what's happening with the stock market. Just like the ringing of the bell to signal the opening of the New York market, each day the glowing spheres break out of a cube arrangement, flying upward to signify the opening of trading. Once "awake," the spheres form patterns based on the market that can be observed throughout the building. At the end of each day's trading, the balls fall back into their cube arrangement, and an animated arrow using the blue LEDs inside the spheres points up or down to show how the stock market performed on that particular day.

The spheres can be formed into many different shapes, including words for special occasions.

Summary

As our devices and applications become more powerful, they also need to become smarter and more clever. They need to harness their own power, performing multiple tasks instead of single ones to improve themselves and users' experience with them. They need to adapt to users—and users to them. Their designers need to become sophisticated about revealing their seams so that users can find unexpected uses for devices. And devices need to become context aware and more sensitive to human attention limits, demanding less of our time and awareness. Interaction designers are the ones who will make this happen.

8

Service Design

In San Francisco, if you want to buy a monthly pass to ride the local public transportation system, MUNI, there are only two ways to do it: either find (via the Web site or, seemingly, by randomly guessing) the stores that sell the pass, or buy it online and have it mailed to you. This plan has (at least) two flaws: very often the passes don't arrive at the stores in time for the beginning of the month, and buying a pass online costs an extra $10 so that the monthly pass offers no savings at all to most commuters. Compared to New York City's MetroCard vending machines (**Figure 8.1**), or to Hong Kong's Octopus SmartCards, which not only allow passage on transportation systems but also work on everything from vending machines to public swimming pools, the MUNI system is terrible. It is a poorly designed service.

When people think of interaction design (if they do at all), they tend to think of it as tied to technology: Web sites, mobile phones, software. I'm as guilty as anyone—the subtitle of this book refers to the creation of applications and devices after all. But technological wonders aren't all interaction designers create. The new frontier of interaction design is services.

Figure 8.1

New York City's MetroCard kiosks are excellent examples of good use of technology in services. Designed by Antenna Design, they are a welcome addition to the New York subway service.

Up until this point in this book, we have been using the clunky phrase "products and services" to describe what interaction designers design without ever much explaining what a service is. Back in Chapter 1, we noted that interaction designers can design not only objects (things) and not only digital or physical things, but also the ephemeral—ways of performing tasks that are hard to pin down but easy to feel. These "ways of performing tasks" are services.

What Is a Service?

A service is a chain of activities that form a process and have value for the end user. You engage in a service when you get your shoes shined or your nails manicured or when you visit a fast-food restaurant. Your mobile phone's usage plan is a service, and you participate in a service every time you travel on a plane, train, or taxi. Services can be small and discrete, such as the sale of postage stamps by some ATM machines, or they can be huge, such as the sorting and delivery of physical mail. Service providers are all around us and account for an enormous portion of the world economy: from restaurants and bars to dry cleaners, hospitals, construction companies, street cleaners, and even complete governments. Services are everywhere.

Services greatly affect our quality of life because we are touched by so many of them every day. A poor service can make your subway ride to work uncomfortable, your packages late or undelivered, your lunch distasteful, your mobile phone coverage poor, and your ability to find evening TV shows problematic.

Service design, like systems design (see Chapter 2), focuses on context—on the entire system of use. People use products (often with others) in environments in structured processes. Service design, really, is designing this whole system of use. The *system* is the service.

The Characteristics of a Service

Most services have many of the following characteristics:

▶ **Intangible.** Although services are often populated with objects, as discussed later in this chapter, the service itself is ephemeral. Customers can't touch or see the service itself—only the physical embodiments of it, such as the food in a restaurant or a firefighter's uniform.

▶   **Provider ownership.** Customers who use a service may come away from it with an owned object such as a cup of coffee or used car, but they don't own the service itself. It cannot be purchased by the customer.

▶   **Co-created.** Services aren't made by the service provider alone; they require the involvement and engagement of the customers as well. Salespeople don't do the shopping for customers (unless asked), waiters don't bring just any food they please, and doctors don't prescribe the same medicine to everyone.

▶   **Flexible.** Although a service must be standardized to some degree, each new situation or customer requires that the service adapt to it. A rude, pushy customer is treated differently than a meek or polite one. When a plane is delayed, the customers and the employees act (and react) differently than when a flight proceeds flawlessly.

▶   **Time based.** Services take time to perform, and that time cannot be recovered if it is lost. Service time that goes unused, such as the time a taxi driver spends looking for passengers, is a missed economic opportunity.

▶   **Active.** Services are created by human labor and are thus difficult to scale. How the people who provide a service act—the customer service, as it is frequently called—can often determine the success or failure of a service.

▶   **Fluctuating demand.** Most services vary by time of day, season, and cultural mood. Hair stylists are overwhelmed during wedding season but are considerably less busy after holidays.

The Elements of Service Design

Traditional design focuses on the relationship between a user and a product. Service design, in contrast, works with multiple *touchpoints*—the store itself, the sign that drew you to the store, the salesperson in the store, what the salesperson says, the packaging the purchased product arrives in—and focuses on users' interaction with these touchpoints *over time*. These touchpoints typically are environments, objects, processes, and people.

Environments

The environment (**Figure 8.2**) is the place where the service takes place. This can be a physical location such as a store or a kiosk, or a digital or intangible location such as a telephone or a Web site. The environment needs to provide the space necessary to perform the actions of the service, as well as cues for those actions, such as signs, posted menus, and displays. The environment tells users what is possible. It creates affordances (see Chapter 3).

Figure 8.2

Supermarkets, like this one in Kenya, have areas designed for the payment of products. One wonders, however, in the age of radio-frequency identification (RFID) tags, which can be embedded in product packaging and possibly allow automatic checkout when the product leaves the store, how much longer this part of the environment will be necessary.

Unlike products, services are often purchased, delivered, and used or consumed in the same place. Thus, the setting for any service needs to contain the resources for purchasing, creating, and consuming the service.

Objects

These resources are often the objects that populate the environment. Objects in service design are meant to be interacted with—the menu at a restaurant, the check-in kiosk in an airport, or the cash register used to ring up a sale. These resources provide the potential for interaction and participation.

Some objects are complex machines, like the baggage sorters at airports (only a portion of which are visible to passengers; see **Figure 8.3**). Others are as simple as a cloth to clean up spills.

Figure 8.3

Objects in services can be huge, complex machines, such as the CrisBag baggage handling system from FKI Logistex, which uses RFID-tagged baggage totes to sort, track, and trace baggage.

Processes

The process is *how* the service is acted out: how it is ordered, created, and delivered (**Figure 8.4**). Everything down to the words used can be designed ("Do you want fries with that?" or "For 25 cents more, you can supersize it"). Processes can be very simple and short—the customer puts money on the newsstand counter and takes a newspaper—or they can be very complicated—the vendor orders newspapers, the vendor pays for newspapers, the newspapers are bundled and shipped daily from printing presses and delivered to individual vendors.

Processes aren't fixed. Customers can be exposed to multiple, varied experiences via repeated exposure to the service. The process can subtly or radically change from place to place or over time. Moreover, there are often multiple pathways through a service; there isn't usually one way to do anything—people are simply too messy for that. Designers have to give up control (or, really, the *myth* of control) when designing a service process. Designers can't control the entire experience.

Figure 8.4
Workers installing a concrete floor follow a set process.

However, interaction designers do have to define and design at least some of the pathways through the service. These pathways contain service moments—small parts of the experience—which, when hung together, constitute the service and its experience.

People

People are an essential part of most services because only through people do most services come alive, usually through complex choreography. In service design, there are two sets of users to design for: the customers and the employees. Customers and employees often perform different parts of the service for the purpose of achieving a particular result. For example, in a Starbucks, customers order their drinks, employees then make the drinks, and then customers customize the drinks, adding milk, sugar, and so on. The two user groups co-create the service *in real time*.

This real-time collaboration to create services means that services are tricky to design and the stakes are high. Failure happens face to face and can cause anger and embarrassment from both customers and employees. Designers, being divine beings only in their own minds, cannot create people; they can only, like a playwright, create *roles* for people within services, such as waiter, chef, or greeter (**Figure 8.5**), and give them parts to play. As Marshall McLuhan told us 40 years ago, people are focused on roles, not goals. Roles have a cluster of tasks surrounding them ("I take the product specifications to the engineers") that are easy to specify and that have traits and skills associated with them, so they are easy to "cast" ("must be a people person").

Figure 8.5

Chefs have clearly defined roles to play in restaurants and catering services and often have uniforms such as this one. Their skills and tasks— prepare and cook food—are also well defined.

Why Design Services?

One of the best reasons for designing services is that services, more easily than most physical products, can be designed to be environmentally good. Making fewer things, especially fewer useless things, is good for the planet. What if, rather than everyone owning a car (especially in crowded urban environments), we shared cars, using them only when necessary? That's the premise of car sharing services such as Zipcar (**Figure 8.6**), where subscribers to the service check out cars for a period of time, returning them to shared parking lots, where others can then check them out.

Figure 8.6

Zipcars allow people to share cars. In urban environments, where owning a car is often burdensome, Zipcars provide an alternative.

Another practical reason for designing services well is simply that good service makes good business. Certainly a poor service can survive if there is no or little competition. Would the Department of Motor Vehicles be such a horrible service if drivers could get their licenses elsewhere? People have shown that they will pay extra for unusual and unusually well-executed services. Even a slightly better service will cause people to seek it out and pay for it. Airlines, for instance, have taken advantage of this with business- and first-class service (**Figure 8.7**). Budget airlines like JetBlue have noticed that fliers will seek them out if the experience of flying with them is much better than that of flying with most of their competitors. All other things (price, convenience, and so on) being equal, their service has become their differentiator in the marketplace.

Figure 8.7

Virgin Airlines spends a considerable amount of time and effort on service design, and it shows. The airline's posh amenities for even coach-class travelers have other airlines scrambling to catch up.

Services and Branding

Interaction designers can't design services without taking full account of branding. Indeed, one of the roots of service design is the "total brand experience" movement of the past two decades, in which marketers and brand managers try to make sure that every time a customer interacts with a company, they have a consistent, branded experience. While that is an interesting goal that still plays out for companies such as Nike (**Figure 8.8**), it starts from a different point of view than does service design: namely, from the *company's* point of view. Total brand experience asks, How can the company imprint itself on the customer? Service design, in contrast, asks, How can the *customer's* experience with the company be a positive one (and thus strengthen the brand)?

Figure 8.8

Nike's Web site reflects its careful attention to brand. Nike's stores, Web site, advertising, and packaging all convey the company's distinctive brand message.

Branding boils down to two elements: the characteristics of the company or organization and the way in which those characteristics are given expression. Tiffany's blue box, the Disney handwriting script, and the green of John Deere are all expressions of brand. In designing services, interaction designers have to figure out how the brand translates in each of the aspects of the service design: environments, objects, processes, and people. This translation is particularly challenging when designing processes, since these are often intangible. You wouldn't create a dainty, fussy check-out process for Home Depot, for example, because it would go against the company's rugged, no-nonsense branding.

In service design, brand can be designed into small details that can have power to delight. In upscale hotels during the room clean-up service, the end of the toilet paper roll is often folded into a neat triangle; this small moment lets the customer know the level of care being provided. When designing services, interaction designers should strive to give users something extra that reflects the company's branding.

The Differences Between Services and Products

Thanks to technology, our products and services are intertwined as never before. We subscribe to phone services to use our mobile phones. We pay to connect our devices to the Internet. We order goods online that are delivered to our homes, and withdraw money from our banks via machines.

Most services are chock-full of products—a fact sometimes overlooked in discussions of service design. Signage, physical devices, Web sites, phone services, lighting, and so on are all part of a typical modern service ecology. The corner store has signs, counters, display shelves, and probably even a Web site. Many of these are specialized products made specifically for that service (**Figure 8.9**). The TiVo box, for example, is a specialized product that you have to buy before you can even use the TiVo service, which provides not only the TV listings, but also the TiVo operating system. (Imagine subscribing to Microsoft Windows.)

Figure 8.9

A very clever map, using the otherwise wasted space of a utility box, designed for that particular box as part of a tourism service for the city of Victoria, British Columbia.

Services, however, have different emotional resonances with users than do individual products. While users may strongly like a service such as TiVo, the attachment that forms to a service is different than that to a physical product. For one thing, services are intangible and likely to change. Services mutate, stagnate, and shift depending on the people supplying them and the business rules that guide them. The experiences at McDonald's and Starbucks can vary wildly, and those businesses both have very controlled service processes.

Shelley Evenson on Service Design

Shelley Evenson is an associate professor and director of graduate studies at Carnegie Mellon University's School of Design. Prior to her academic career, she was vice president and chief experience strategist for Scient, director of design at DKA/Digital Knowledge Assets, director at Doblin Group, and vice president of Fitch. She has published a number of articles and presented papers at numerous conferences on design languages in hypermedia, interaction design, design research, and service design.

Why is service design important?

According to one IBM report, today more than 70 percent of the U.S. labor force is engaged in service delivery. New technology has enabled internationally tradable services. We are at a tipping point. A huge portion of the economy is now focused on knowledge-based information services. I believe that as we shift to this service-centered society, it won't be good enough to view services from a purely management or operations-based perspective. Companies will need to turn to service design and innovation to differentiate themselves in increasingly competitive markets and to create opportunities that address new challenges in the service sector.

How is designing a service different from designing a product?

When designing a product, much of the focus is on mediating the interaction between the person and the artifact. Great product designers consider more of the context in their design. In service design, designers must create resources that connect people to people, people to machines, and machines to machines. You must consider the environment, the channel, the touchpoint. Designing for service becomes a systems problem and often even a system of systems challenges. The elements or resources that designers need to create to mediate the interactions must work on all these levels and at the same time facilitate connections that are deeply personal, open to participation and change, and drop-dead stunning.

Shelley Evenson on Service Design *Continued*

What can interaction designers bring to the design of services?

Interaction designers use methods in their process that can be directly applied to service design. Immersive ethnographic methods can help designers account for the complexity of service elements that are onstage, backstage, visible, and invisible in the service experience. We add a kind of theater or enactment to our service process. Enactment is when first the development team and then participants from the delivery organization act out the service experience with specific roles and rough props. I've seen this technique become more popular with interaction designers in recent days. Developing constituent archetypes or personas is also useful in service design since the characters can be used to drive service scenarios before they are enacted. Nearly all the methods introduced in this book could apply.

What fields are most in need of service design right now?

I believe there are loads of opportunity in health care. The model for service delivery hasn't changed much in the last 50 years. Medical research and technology have advanced beyond what the model can account for. Additionally, people's expectations for service have changed. Today we have endless access to information, self-service everything, and overnight delivery. These new expectations are finally hitting the medical profession. Some institutions are responding, most notably the Mayo Clinic and UPMC.

Another area of opportunity is software. I think people are just beginning to look beyond the metaphor of software as product, to seeing the potential of product/service systems, or even systems of systems, as new means of framing company offerings. Financial services are another area of opportunity.

Where do you see service design headed in the near future?

Europeans have been seriously thinking about service design for at least 10 years. They've made a lot of progress, especially with regard to designing for service experiences that encourage more responsible product ownership and sustainable lifestyles. We could begin to see some of those efforts cross over to the U.S.

I also believe we will begin to see more business strategists looking forward toward experience in designing for service instead of backward toward products. When this happens, we may see a demand for service designers that rivals what happened for interaction designers in the Internet boom days.

I own a Zippo lighter that belonged to my grandfather. Barring catastrophe, that Zippo will always be the same. It's tangible: I can touch it, use it, see it easily. Not so with services, especially digital services, many of which change frequently. And, truth be told, customers can easily switch services as well. If an auction service better than eBay came along, users would switch. Even if my grandfather had used eBay, that probably wouldn't stop me from changing to a new service if something better came along. But I won't trade in my grandfather's Zippo for something better. I have an attachment to it. It's sentimental, sure, but humans are emotional creatures and don't always make logical decisions. The point is that people, probably because of their biological wiring, more easily form emotional attachments to things than to intangible services.

Note *There are certainly products—many products—that we don't notice, enjoy, or have an attachment to: namely, those that are poorly designed, difficult to use, ugly, or simply dated. Services that replace these products, such as TiVo, which provides much more convenience than traditional television sets, are certainly appreciated and welcomed.*

On the Internet, it's practically impossible to separate product design from service design. Most noncontent Web sites provide services delivered over the Internet instead of in person. Google, eBay, Yahoo, online brokerages and banks, travel sites, and so on all provide services or are part of larger services that combine both online and offline products, as in the case of Netflix, which has both a Web site for ordering DVDs and mailers (**Figure 8.10**) for sending and returning them. Users don't own the Web site (obviously)—they just use the service—which makes most Web services vulnerable. If a search engine that was better than Google came along would you use it? You might. This is one of the reasons why companies like Google and Yahoo give users digital objects like toolbars. It's easier to switch services than it is to get rid of a thing, even a digital thing.

Figure 8.10

The current Netflix mailer, introduced in early 2005. The result of more than five years of experimentation, this mailer transports approximately 1.4 million DVDs a day to Netflix's 4.2 million subscribers.

The Craft of Service Design

Because service design itself is new, the service design process is still being developed. But interaction designers who work in service design have methods they use to craft services, in addition to most of the techniques described in Chapter 5. These methods have been developed by service design consultancies such as IDEO and Live|Work and by designers such as Shelley Evenson (see the interview in this chapter).

Note   *The business community, too, has spent considerable time and effort thinking about services. Interaction designers working in service design should draw upon this community's experience while bringing to the table the approaches and methods of design (see Chapter 2 and Chapter 5).*

Environment Description

Before starting the design of a service, designers need to know as much as they can about where the service will be located (or is located already). An environment description details the location as much as possible. Maps, diagrams, blueprints, photographs, screenshots, and videos can all be part of an environment description. Photographs with annotations (**Figure 8.11**) are excellent for environment descriptions.

Figure 8.11

Annotated photographs from a project done with the Carnegie Library of Pittsburgh by MAYA.

Stakeholder Description

As discussed earlier, the users of services are both customers and employees. But services, because they often live in a physical context, affect more than just their direct users. A change to a bus route may, for instance, affect thousands who never take the bus: the newsstand that depends on the riders for business, drivers in cars, the people living on the bus route, city officials, taxi drivers who compete with the service, and so on. The designer needs to identify both the obvious and the nonobvious stakeholders who are affected by the service.

Designers may have to make some difficult choices in regards to these stakeholders. The new service may be better than what currently exists, but at what cost? How many mom-and-pop stores has Wal-Mart driven out of business? How many local coffee shops has Starbucks ruined? Designers often need to prioritize the stakeholders. A hard fact of designing is that the neighbor down the street is often less important than the customer. Services can have a human cost that designers need to consider.

Company Perceptions and Branding

Unless a service is new and for a new company, customers will likely have expectations about how the service will work based on the company's brand and their own experiences with the company. Designers need to be aware of these expectations and to design the service appropriately. Designers also need to ask frankly whether this service is appropriate for the company, or how it can be made appropriate. Some companies and brands such as Virgin Group, Ltd., seem infinitely flexible, with services running the gamut from online music downloading to space travel—but most aren't. If BMW suddenly wanted to offer health care services, you'd have to wonder if the CEO went off his medication.

Designers also need to figure out what the company is good at so that any new service draws on those strengths. If a company is known for its great customer service, as Southwest Airlines is, the designer would be foolish not to capitalize on that.

Touchpoints

Designers need to compile a list of all the touchpoints to understand what raw materials they have to work with or need to create. These touchpoints can include (and certainly aren't limited to) any of the following:

▸   Physical locations

▸   Specific parts of locations

▸   Signage

▸   Objects

▸   Web sites

▸   Mailings (e-mail and regular)

▸   Spoken communication

▸   Printed communications (receipts, maps, tickets, and so on)

▸   Applications

▸   Machinery

▸   Customer service

▸   Partners

Do these exist already or do they need to be created? Are they well designed or are they trouble spots?

These touchpoints are the raw materials that interaction designers work with. Once the list of existing and potential touchpoints has been created, it can be used to brainstorm designs for each touchpoint.

Touchpoints are used in both the process map and the service blueprint.

Process Map

No service exists in a vacuum. Indeed, many services exist only when connected to other services. For example, the service of ordering a monthly parking pass at a garage makes no sense without the parking service itself. But before starting work on the parking service, the interaction designer needs to see how that part fits into the overall customer pathway, which includes possibly the purchase of a monthly pass. A process map (**Figure 8.12**) provides this overview.

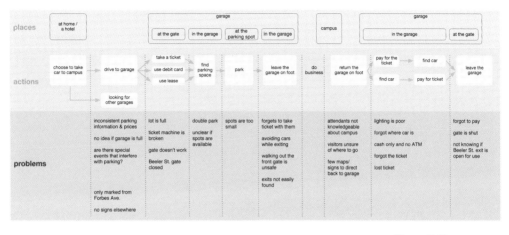

Figure 8.12

Process maps provide an overview of what is to be designed and can indicate problem areas in an existing service.

A process map shows the high-level view of the overall experience and where the design work being done falls in that overall experience. How might a project that designs the service on a plane affect the check-in service? A process map shows the boundaries of the project. While a process map does show steps in the process similar to a task flow (see Chapter 5), one major difference is that a process map can also show the surrounding steps that are not going to be designed.

Process maps should also indicate the touchpoints at each stage of the process. When checking in at an airport, for example, the touchpoints include the human agent, the kiosk, the ticket, the ticket sleeve, and the counter.

A process map can also point out areas of trouble and missed opportunities. Perhaps a crucial step in the process is missing or poorly designed. Perhaps there aren't enough touchpoints to complete the users' tasks. These issues get addressed in the service blueprint.

Service Blueprint

Much as wireframes are key documents for digital products (see Chapter 5), service blueprints (**Figure 8.13**) are critical documents for services. Service blueprints present two major elements: service moments and the service string.

Figure 8.13

A piece of a service blueprint, part of the MAYA Carnegie Library of Pittsburgh project. Service blueprints show not only discrete moments in the service, but also how those moments flow together in a service string.

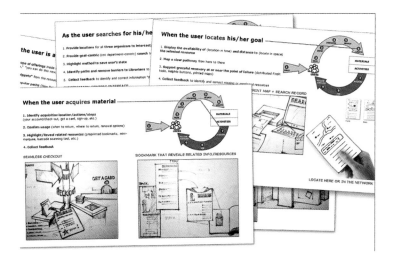

Service Moments

Every service is composed of a set of discrete moments that can be designed. For example, a car wash service has (at least) the following service moments:

▶ Customer finds the car wash.

▶ Customer enters the car wash.

▶ Customer chooses what to have done (just washing, waxing, and so on).

▶ Customer pays.

▶ Car moves into the car wash.

▶ Car is washed.

▶ Car is dried.

▶ Interior of the car is cleaned.

▶ Customer leaves the car wash.

Each of these moments can be designed, right down to how the nozzles spray water onto the car. The service blueprint should include all of these moments and present designs for each one. And since there can be multiple paths through a service, there can be multiple designs for each moment. In the car wash scenario, perhaps there are multiple ways of finding the car wash: signs, advertisements, a barker on the street, fliers, and so on.

Here, the list of touchpoints can come into play. Which touchpoint is or could be used during each service moment? For each service moment, the touchpoints should be designed. In our car wash example, for instance, the customer paying moment probably has at least two touchpoints: a sign listing the washing services available and their costs, and some sort of machine or human attendant who takes the customer's money. All of these elements— what the sign says and how it says it, how the machine operates (Does it accept credit cards? How does it make change?), what the attendant says and does—can be designed. A major part of the service blueprint should be the brainstormed ideas for each touchpoint at each service moment. Each service moment should have a concept attached to it, such as the sketches in Figure 8.13 showing a possible check-out kiosk and a bookmark for related library information.

Ideally, each moment should have a sketch or photograph or other rendering of the design, similar to single storyboard frames.

For each service moment, the service blueprint should show what service elements are affected: the environment, objects, processes, and people involved. Designers should especially look for service moments that can deliver high value for a low cost. Sometimes small, low-cost changes or additions to a service can quickly provide high value to users. For instance, some airlines found that passengers want a drink as soon as they board the plane. But because other passengers are still boarding and in the aisle, flight attendants can't offer drink service at that time. The solution was to put a cooler with water bottles at the front of the plane, so that passengers, if they want, can get a drink as they board—a low-cost, high-value solution.

Service String

The second component of a service blueprint is the service string. The service string shows the big idea for the service in written and visual form, usually in the form of storyboards (see Chapter 5). Designers create service strings by putting concepts for various service moments together to form a scenario, or string, of events that provide a pathway through the service.

The service string demonstrates in a vivid way what the pathways through the service will be and provides a comprehensive, big-picture view of the new service. Viewers can see how customers order, pay for, and receive the service, and how employees provide the service. For example, a service string for the earlier car wash example would show in a single scenario customers seeing the new signs, customers using the new machine to pay for the car wash, the special washing service, the attendants who hand-dry the cars, and the new vacuum for cleaning out the cars after they are washed.

Service Prototype

Prototyping a service usually isn't much like prototyping a product. Since both the process and people are so important to services, services don't really come alive until people are using the service and walking through the process. Prototyping a service typically involves creating scenarios based on the service moments outlined in the service blueprint and acting them out with clients and stakeholders, playing out the scenarios as theatre.

Role playing constitutes a significant part of the service design process. Only through enactments can designers really determine how the service will feel. Someone (often the designer) is cast in the role of employee, while others play the roles of customers. This prototyping can make use of a script or an outline of a script, or the enactments can simply be improvised. The players act their way through a service string to demonstrate how the service works.

Figure 8.14

A prototype of a service design environment, created by projecting images behind the designers/ actors.

Ideally, these scenarios will be played within a mock-up of the environment (**Figure 8.14**), with prototypes of the objects involved as well. Only in this way can the flow and feel of the service really be known. Environments can be simulated using giant foam blocks for objects, masking tape on the floor to block out areas, images projected on walls, and so on.

Services, as with beta software, also can be prototyped using a live environment with real customers and employees. The Mayo Clinic's SPARC program does this (see the case study that follows), as do many retail stores, using what are called pilot programs at a small number of locations. These prototypes are, of course, extremely high fidelity, working exactly as the actual service would because they involve actual customers. Although it is certainly best to start with low-fidelity service prototypes (if only because of the cost), eventually the service will need to be tested with actual customers and employees, either in a prototype/pilot environment or live, making adjustments as the service lives.

Case Study: Electronic Check-In System

The Company

The Mayo Clinic, an internationally known medical facility.

The Problem

Most patient satisfaction with health care comes through the delivery of that care, not necessarily the care's effectiveness. Designers at the Mayo Clinic observed that a point of patient annoyance is the check-in process. The check-in process sometimes even exacerbates medical conditions.

The Process

The Mayo Clinic's SPARC (See, Plan, Act, Refine, Communicate) program was created to fix just such a problem as the check-in process. SPARC provides live-environment (real patients, real doctors) exploration and experimentation to support the design and development of innovations in health-care delivery. SPARC is both a physical space and a methodology combining design and scientific rigor. Embedded within a clinical practice in the hospital, the SPARC space has modular furniture and movable walls that allow many different configurations, and it is staffed with a blend of physicians, business professionals, and designers. Using the airline industry as a model, SPARC designed a prototype of a check-in kiosk, collected initial feedback from potential users, and then iteratively refined that prototype.

Case Study: Electronic Check-In System *Continued*

SPARC prototyped with paper and on a laptop before creating the kiosk.

The Solution

SPARC designed a self-check-in service similar to airline check-in services at airports. Patients check in using a kiosk instead of waiting in a line just to say that they have arrived. SPARC tested the kiosk with 100 patients and found a high rate of acceptance and significant reduction in the number of unnecessary interactions required while the patient was waiting for service. There was also a marked reduction in patients' waiting time.

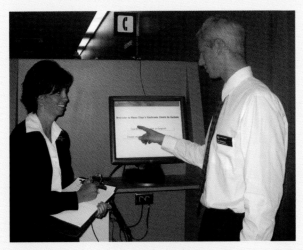

The finished version of the kiosk check-in system.

@ the Center of Digital Services

You certainly can't replicate customers or employees, but digital services, espe-cially Web services, are easier to replicate than the content that powers them.

My new law, Saffer's Law, is this: *It's easier to create the form of a digital service than it is to create the content (products) in that service.*

Hundreds of news aggregators can grab content from *The New York Times*, but creating the content of *The New York Times* is much harder. It probably wouldn't be difficult (at least on the front end) to make a better auction service than eBay; the trick would be to move eBay's millions of users (and products) over to it. eBay itself is now trying to do this with eBay Express (**Figure 8.15**).

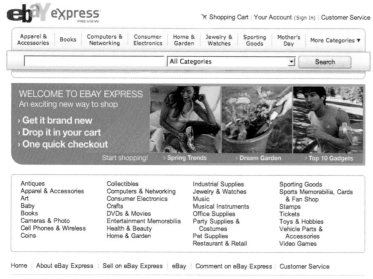

Figure 8.15

eBay Express is an attempt to add a new interface to the eBay auction service.

Certainly, as this chapter has discussed, designing (and constantly main-taining and upgrading) a great service is no easy task. And at the center of most Web services is a kernel of content. This can be user supplied, such as the photos on Flickr, or employee supplied, such as video from CNN. But that content has to be good or the service is junk. You wouldn't trade using an online brokerage firm if the company's stock quotes were bad. You wouldn't go to Google if its search results were terrible. And you wouldn't shop on eBay if there was nothing to buy. (Just ask Amazon Auctions.)

To a lesser extent, too, at the center of most offline services is a product, and if the product is terrible, unless there is no competition or the price extremely low, even the greatest service isn't going to save it for long. If Starbucks' coffee was undrinkable, people wouldn't continue to buy it. If an airline always lost its passengers' luggage, you wouldn't fly that airline.

In their quest to make a great service, designers should take care to ensure that the content or product around which the service is built is worthwhile lest the whole effort be for naught.

Summary

Increasingly, interaction designers are involved (sometimes without even knowing it) in service design. The introduction of new technology such as RFID tags and mobile devices into services makes this inevitable as the traditional designers of services—the service providers and business consultants—turn to interaction designers for their expertise in bridging the gap between technology and people. This is a good thing. Services are too often created as though the humans engaged with them are an afterthought. Applying interaction design techniques to these processes that are all around us can lead to a richer, more humanistic world.

9

The Future of Interaction Design

The future of interaction design is being created right now. Interaction designers on their own or at start-up companies or huge organizations are devising products and services that will change how we interact with each other and with our world. It's not hyperbole to suggest that the next 20 years will see significant changes in almost all aspects of our lives: our health care experience, how we entertain ourselves, how we shop, how we get from place to place. How, when, and where we receive information will be completely transformed, and interaction designers will be there, to guide and design the products and services that will shape the future.

Interaction designers must take a role not only in creating the future of the discipline, but also making sure that the future works well and is designed for humans to use and enjoy. The next decades will see some amazing advances, some of which are explored in this chapter, and interaction designers will be at the center of all of it. It's an exciting time.

In the next decade, the Internet will move from behind computer monitors to the objects and buildings that are all around us. Microprocessors, sensors, and radio-frequency identification (RFID) tags will be built into everyday objects and networked, creating what writer Bruce Sterling calls "an Internet of things." Indeed, we will likely stop thinking of the Internet as a destination or a place, just as we don't think of electricity as such.

With wireless connections blanketing our cities (either through monolithic engineering projects such as Google's current wireless project in San Francisco or ad-hoc networks patched together by individuals and businesses), the ability to access information contextually, when and where it is needed, will become more commonplace. We will be able to find people and things, and they will be able to find us.

As described in Chapter 7, our products and services will better adapt to us, and we to them. Robots will perform tasks in our homes, schools, cities, and businesses. Intelligent agents will find information we need before we need it. We will wear our computers on our sleeves, if the computer isn't the sleeve itself.

The future will be what the future has always been: hopeful, scary, unknown, disorienting. Only more so.

The Next 10 Years of the Internet

"I live in Walled City," he said.

"Mitsuko told me. That's like a multi-user domain."

"Walled City is unlike anything."

"Give me the address when I give you the emulator. I'll check it out."
The sidewalk arched over a concrete channel running with grayish
water. It reminded her of her Venice. She wondered if there had
been a stream there once.

"It has no address," he said.

"That's impossible," Chia said.

He said nothing.

—From *Idoru* by William Gibson

Over the next decade, there will be a wide range of products and services online, from highly structured to nearly formless. The more "traditional," structured products—blogs, home pages, marketing and communication sites, content sites, search engines, and so on—will have their form and content determined mainly by their designers and creators.

Less structured products will be rich, desktop-like applications, the more interesting of which will be Internet native and built to take advantage of the strengths of the Internet: collective actions and data (Amazon's "People who bought this also bought..."), social communities across wide distances (Yahoo Groups), aggregation of many sources of data (Google News), near real-time access to timely data (Morningstar stock quotes), and easy publishing of content from one to many (blogs, Flickr). For many of these products and services, it is the users who supply the content (such as it is).

And there will also be a new set of products and services, many of which won't have associated Web sites to visit at all. Instead, there will be loose collections of application parts, content, and data that don't exist in a fixed location, yet can be located, used, reused, fixed, and remixed. The content people will search for and use may reside on an individual computer, a mobile phone, or traffic sensors along a remote highway. Users won't need to know where these loose bits live; instead, their tools will know.

Tools for the Next Web

These unstructured bits won't be useful without the tools and the knowledge necessary to make sense of them, similar to the way an HTML file doesn't make much sense without a browser to view it. Indeed, many of these bits will be inaccessible or hidden if a user doesn't have the right tools.

This is where interaction designers come in: creating tools for the next generations of the Internet. The tools we'll use to find, read, filter, use, mix, remix, and connect us to the Internet will have to be a lot smarter and do a lot more work than the ones we have now.

Part of that work is in formatting. Who and what determines how something looks and works? With the unstructured bits of content and functionality, perhaps only a veneer of form will remain. How something looks will be an uneasy mix of the data and the tools we use to engage with it. Indeed, visual design is becoming centralized in the tools and methods we use to view and interact with content, moving away from its decentralized locations on Web sites. Already RSS readers let users customize the way they view feeds from a variety of sources. Soon, expect to see this type of customization happening with bits of functionality as well as content.

Web browsers will probably be the elements most affected by these new, varied experiences. Our current browsers were designed for navigating a hypertext content space—structured products and services, in other words. They are poor to merely adequate for Web applications, and nearly useless for unstructured products and services. We will need new browsers—new tools altogether—and interaction designers need to be involved in creating them.

It would also be a mistake to think that most of these tools will be on laptop or desktop computers. According to some researchers, the number of people accessing the Internet will quadruple from the current 500 million to 2 billion people by 2010—half of them using cheap mobile devices as their means of access (**Figure 9.1**). The shift away from desktop-like experiences will be profound and require incredible amounts of work from interaction designers to become a reality.

It is more important now than ever before that our digital tools have the characteristics of good interaction design baked into them. These tools will determine what we can do online and how we can do it and what it will feel like. Our online experiences will largely be determined by how good these tools are, in much the same way the first 10 years of the Web were shaped by the browsers we used to view it.

Figure 9.1

A woman using a mobile phone that is part of a phone-sharing service offered in Ulan Bataar in Mongolia.

Intelligent Agents

Some of these tools will likely be software acting on our behalf. These "intelligent agents" will be a type of application that resides in (and sometimes follows its user between) digital devices. The duty of these agents will be to perform tasks that are impossible or too time consuming for humans, such as finding, sorting, and filtering every blog post about interaction design ever posted or constantly monitoring networks for problems. These agents will monitor our behavior (which is why some call them "myware," a riff on "spyware") and gather and use information for us before we need it. They will watch over our devices, our homes, and even our physical health.

What's being called the *semantic Web* will help fulfill this prediction. Currently, Web pages are mostly designed to be read by people, not machines. The semantic Web would change this, so that software including intelligent agents can use the Internet more effectively. Using the semantic Web, for example, an agent could find the restaurant closest to your current location and make a reservation based on your schedule.

Of course, having semi-autonomous agents roaming the Web doing things that the user may be only dimly aware of (if at all) is a frightening prospect. Users will want to make sure that these agents aren't doing the wrong things on their behalf. The interaction designers who will be involved in creating these agents will also have to design the means for users to supervise and control their agents. This is a design challenge still waiting to be fully explored.

Spimes and the Internet of Things

Novelist-cum-design-critic Bruce Sterling has predicted that in the future, interaction designers will be creating and working with a type of object that he calls a *spime*. Spimes are networked, context-aware, self-monitoring, self-documenting, uniquely identified objects that exude data about themselves and their environments. Spimes reveal every piece of metadata (their location, their owner, the date they were made, usage patterns, and so on) about themselves. They can be tracked through space (the "sp-" part of the term) and time (the "-ime" part) throughout their entire life cycles, from their prototyping to their eventual destruction.

These spimes will likely have RFID tags that identify them and allow them to communicate. Using sensors and wireless technology, they will communicate with each other and the Internet like a swarm. People will be able to locate and modify spimes and other similarly enabled objects and to add information to them, such as "These are my shoes."

Spimes will create an informational Web: the Internet of things, the uses (and abuses) for which boggle the mind. Imagine having a list of every item in your house, down to the smallest pack of matches. Lose your mobile phone in a taxi? Simply find where it is in real time.

Note   Of course, the privacy issues related to an Internet of things boggle the mind as well. Imagine thieves being able to find all the most expensive items within several blocks, or governments being able easily and instantly to see who you just called on your phone.

The data that this Internet of things will reveal will be fascinating and frightening. Sterling uses the example of tennis shoes. Spime tennis shoes, over time, could reveal what happens to their rubber soles at the end of their life cycle: are they being recycled into playground coverings or are they becoming aerosol carcinogens? Using this data, we will be able to see with clarity the impact of products on our world. Spimes offer the possibility of accountability in products.

As designers such as Adam Greenfield (see the interview later in this chapter) have noted, what is missing from the idea of an Internet of things (or at least from the nomenclature) is *people*. How do people work with and affect an Internet of things? While things may have meaning in and of themselves, they derive (at least) an additional layer of meaning when used by people. How interaction designers place human beings into the Internet of things is a challenge for the future.

Transmedia Interactions

We are starting to see content cross between media channels as never before, and interaction designers will frequently have to work in these different channels. Famously, music has spread from stereos to computers to MP3 players. I can now watch TV shows on my television set, computer, and iPod.

New content increasingly is being created to take advantage of the strengths and weaknesses of the various media channels. Viewers can text message to vote on game shows like *American Idol*. The TV show *Lost* assumes that viewers will be watching on a TiVo device or an iPod with the ability to freeze frames and that they will then discuss these frames in online forums. Some content is conceived with transmedia properties—Pokemon, for instance, inhabits games, movies, TV shows, Web sites, and so on, ad nauseum.

This transmedia experience finds its fullest expression in what are being called alternate reality games (ARGs). ARGs are frequently used to promote movies; for instance, the ARG *The Beast* promoted the movie *A.I.*, and the ARG *Metacortechs* promoted the *Matrix* movies. ARGs deliberately blur the line between what is in the game and what isn't, typically by pointing users to multiple Web sites, some of which are real and some of which aren't. These Web sites are usually where main game "play" happens, although many games also use e-mail, instant messaging, and text and voice messages to supplement or enhance the game play (see the Perplex City case study).

Case Study: Perplex City

The Company

Mind Candy Design

The Problem

Mind Candy Design wanted to create a game that would cross many types of media (Internet, television, mobile phones, newspapers, and so on) and could be played globally by thousands of people simultaneously over a long time period.

The Solution

Perplex City is a hybrid collectible-card game and alternate reality game (ARG) whose goal is to locate a stolen object. The object is real, hidden somewhere in the world, and the game offers a real $200,000 reward to the player who finds it. Players buy packs of six cards (there are 260 total cards), each of which has a puzzle on the front. The puzzles include riddles, origami challenges, pop-culture trivia, logical mindbenders, 3D mazes, and Egyptian hieroglyphs. Players can assemble many of the cards together, creating large maps or new puzzles. These puzzles range from very simple to incredibly intricate.

A set of Perplex City cards. The cards provide clues to puzzles and can, when put together, make larger puzzles.

Case Study: Perplex City *Continued*

The game crosses media like few others have: sometimes a puzzle directs players to fake corporate Web sites or to blogs that contain other clues. Players may need to send text messages to get information, or check the classified ads of newspapers in China, or, in one case, become a published author in order to gain access to a research library that contains critical information! Players enter answers at the Perplex City Web site, where they earn points for correct answers and can compare their rankings to those of other players.

An example of a "fake" Web site for Perplex City, which has clues for solving one of the game's puzzles.

Human-Robot Interactions

Robots are no longer the science-fiction machines of yore, nor are they used only to create cars in factories. Robots—broadly defined as programmable machines that can perform specific physical tasks—are among us, likely for good. A robot, however, is more than just an object. It is both a product and a service.

The South Korean Ministry of Information and Communication predicts that by 2020, every household in South Korea will have a robot. While other countries have focused on robots for military or industrial use, South Korea is developing networked robots for services like babysitting, cleaning, and security. As early as 2007, these robots are scheduled to be on the market.

But it's not only South Korea that will see an influx of robots; robots are being designed and built all over the globe: as floor cleaners (**Figure 9.2**), toys (**Figure 9.3**), musical instruments (**Figure 9.4**), and more. Because of the complex issues surrounding robots, from the emotional to the technical, interaction designers need to become more involved in their creation and use.

Figure 9.2

iRobot's Scooba is a floor-washing robot that can prep, wash, scrub, and dry hard floors, all at the touch of a button.

Figure 9.3
Lego Mindstorms allow children and hobbyists to create sophisticated robots easily.

Figure 9.4
ForestBot is a robotic installation by the music/technology group League of Electronic Musical Urban Robots (LEMUR). ForestBot is a collection of 25 ten-foot stalks that each have an egg-shaped rattle mounted on the free end.

Interaction designers need to be aware of two factors when designing robots: autonomy and social interaction. Autonomy is the robot's ability to act on the user's behalf. Robots like those of Lego Mindstorms have very little autonomy, but some "robots," such as pacemakers and artificial hearts, have full autonomy—their human users don't have to tell them to work.

Figure 9.5

Carnegie Mellon's roboreceptionist gives directions, answers the phone, and even gossips about her "life."

Similarly, there are robots, like the toy Furby, that engage in little reciprocal interaction, and others, like Carnegie Mellon's Valerie, the robot receptionist (**Figure 9.5**), designed specifically to interact with humans.

Robot designer and professor Jodi Forlizzi has outlined three main design issues with robots:

▶ **Form.** Does the robot have a humanlike appearance? How big is it? What are its physical characteristics such as size, shape, scale, and the materials it is made of?

▶ **Function.** How does the robot communicate and express itself? Does it use sound, motion, gesture, light, color, or scent?

▶ **Manner of behavior.** How does the robot behave and in what situations? How does it go about its activities and how does it interact with humans? How social is it?

Carl DiSalvo on Designing for Robots

Carl DiSalvo is currently a post-doctoral fellow with joint appointments in the Center for the Arts in Society and the Studio for Creative Inquiry at Carnegie Mellon University. Previously, Carl worked as a designer for MetaDesign and as a consultant for the Walker Art Center's New Media Initiatives. In 2006, he received a Ph.D. in Design from Carnegie Mellon University. As a graduate student, he worked as a design research associate on the Project on People and Robots at the Human-Computer Interaction Institute.

Briefly describe the realm of robots. What type of robots are being made or planned?

We can make some distinctions among robots, but none of them are mutually exclusive. A robot could, and often does, fall into two or more categories. For example, there are social robots, service robots, and field robots. Many of these distinctions actually relate to the research question at hand more than to a kind of consumer product. This of course reflects the fact that outside of a few domains and a few choice examples, robots still are primarily research endeavors.

The most common domains for contemporary robotic products are military or industrial settings. Robots are also beginning to be used in medicine and scientific exploration. And of course toys. Robots for the home consumer, such as the Roomba, are still uncommon. For example, there are a handful of vacuum and lawn-mowing robots, but other than that, except for toys, there aren't really robots, as we commonly think of them, in the home.

Carl DiSalvo on Designing for Robots *Continued*

What type of design work is being done with robots now?

All kinds. This is what makes robotics so exciting. The challenges and opportunities of robotics sweep across every field of design. Perhaps the most obvious is the work in industrial design in creating the visual form of the robot. The industrial design of a robot is an example of styling visual form with significant impact on interaction. In fact, it's difficult to separate industrial design from interaction design in robots. Because of the newness of robotics and the public's unfamiliarity with robots, the visual form of the robot often takes a precedence in shaping our expectations of the robot and how we interact with the product.

In addition to designing the visual form of the robot, there is a lot of interface design involved with robots: interfaces for tele-operation as well as interfaces for direct interaction. These interfaces might be screen based, physical, voice, or some combination of the three. Because we have yet to arrive at any standards for, or even common experiences of, interacting with a robot interface, interaction design for robotics is open to broad inquiry and invention.

How is designing for robots different from designing other products?

Robots are hyperboles of the products contemporary designers are challenged with. That is, they are an exaggeration of the contemporary products because robots are "everything all at once": complex embodied technological artifacts that require significant design knowledge of industrial, communication, interaction, and service design; potent cultural icons; and, too, the most mundane of gadgets.

All of the diverse elements of a product are brought together and amplified in a robot. This presents a nearly unique challenge and opportunity. Designing robots requires a level of synthesis not often encountered in other products.

What will be the role of interaction designers in this field in the future?

In many ways, robots are still fictional entities, at least when it comes to common consumer products. Interaction designers have the opportunity to invent what these new products of the future might or should be like. This comes along with significant responsibility to shape these products in ways that are not merely seductive but appropriate.

One of the most pressing needs concerning the design of robots, concerning design in general, is to consider how these nascent technologies become products, and in the process to take up the opportunity to critically engage these technologies, rather than simply striving forward with unreflective novelty.

Wearables

The next computer you own might be a size 10.

Although the idea of wearable computing has been around since the early 1960s, it wasn't until 2005, when Adidas introduced Adidas_1 (**Figure 9.6**), a running shoe with a microprocessor in it that adjusts the cushioning of the shoe based on its use, that the idea of wearables reached the public consciousness. Likely, Adidas succeeded because the Adidas_1 looks stylish, unlike many previous attempts at wearables: clunky pieces of gear awkwardly strapped to some geek's body.

Figure 9.6

The Adidas_1 shoe has a magnetic sensor in the heel that senses the level of compression. This compression level is sent to a microprocessor in the shoe that adjusts the cushioning via a motor-driven cable system, making the shoe softer or firmer as needed.

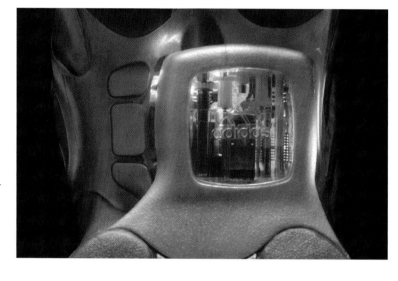

Designers of wearables take as their starting point the fact that the thing most people have with them most of the time is their clothes. Why not, then, use clothing as a platform for technology so that we have things that we need with us all the time? Computers in clothing can adjust the clothing to project messages, react to other devices, or change according to the weather or the wearer's mood (**Figure 9.7**). Of course, wearables don't have to be clothing per se. BodyMedia's SenseWear products (**Figure 9.8**) are small devices that strap on an arm and monitor the wearer's health. Wristwatches have been a basis for wearables, such as Fossil's WristPDA.

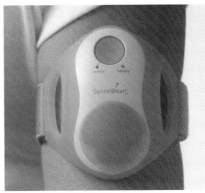

Figure 9.7

F+R Hugs ("The Hug Shirt") created by CuteCircuit is a shirt that allows people to send and receive the physical sensation of a hug over long distances. Embedded in the shirt are sensors that feel the hug's strength, the skin's warmth, and the heartbeat rate of the sender. Actuators re-create those sensations in the shirt of the distant loved one.

Figure 9.8

BodyMedia's SenseWear armband, worn on the back of the upper-right arm, uses a multisensor array to collect continuous physiological data directly from the wearer's skin. Users can monitor their energy expenditure (calories burned), duration of physical activity, number of steps taken, sleep/wake states, and more.

The challenges for interaction designers working with wearables are many, as are the opportunities. Designers have to pay particular attention not only to functionality, but also to form. Wearables, unlike devices that sit on a desk or slip into a pocket or purse, are meant to be, well, *worn*. And things worn on the body for long periods of time need to be durable, stylish, and unobtrusive. Their context is anywhere that humans are, and that is an extremely broad and varied set of environments. The opportunity with wearables is in the fact that people don't need to be concerned about "another device to carry." Users won't have to carry anything except the clothes they wear or something strapped to their bodies like a fashion accessory. Information and functionality move with the user, available when needed, and data is captured from the user's body and location that might never be captured otherwise.

Wearables also allow interaction designers to take advantage of more parts of the body than they are used to engaging. A glove with sensors might unlock doors with a flick of a finger. A sleeve might become a screen for projecting images, and a necklace, like Microsoft Research's proposed SenseCam, might take thousands of pictures a day, allowing users to replay their days visually if they choose.

Ubiquitous Computing

Over the past 60 years, the ratio of humans to computers has been chang-ing. In the early years of computing, the ratio of humans to computers was many to one: many people worked on one mainframe computer. Then came the era of the personal computer, and the ratio changed to one to one: people who used computers had their own on their desks. Recently, however, and in the future this will be even more true, the ratio has changed so that one person now has many "computers" under his or her control: a laptop, digital camera, MP3 player, mobile phone, car, microwave, television, and on and on. In the words of Mark Weiser, the Xerox PARC scientist who wrote the seminal papers on the subject, most of these computers are "invisible, yet all around us."

The era of ubiquitous computing (or *ubicomp*) has, like so much of the "future" technology in this chapter, already started; it just isn't widespread yet. As microprocessors and sensors grow ever cheaper and also more pow-erful, it's easy to imagine the ratio of humans to computers becoming one to thousands. Most of these computers will be embedded in the products we own, and aside from the behavior they afford, they will be imperceptible to us. We won't be controlling them via a keyboard and mouse either. As described in Chapter 6, these interfaces will have no faces; we'll engage with them using voice, touch, and gestures.

Note *Designers have yet to figure out ways of documenting the gestures, voice commands, and body positions that will trigger and engage ubicomp systems. It's been suggested that dance notation or some variation could be used.*

Interaction designers have a major part to play in the design of ubicomp systems, and it will be an exciting and interesting time. The possibilities for interactions between people through ubicomp are simply astounding. While you get ready in the morning, your bathroom mirror might show you your calendar, the weather report for the day, and perhaps e-mail from your friends. The bus stop might indicate when the next bus will arrive and how crowded it is. The bus itself might have digital notes on it left by passengers ("This seat is broken"). At your office, a wall might be your monitor, turn-ing on when you tell it to. Meeting rooms might automatically record what is said and drawn on digital whiteboards. Any room you are in throughout the day might play music of your choice and adjust to the temperature you like based on the clothes you are wearing.

This scenario sounds to us now like science fiction or those old AT&T "You Will" commercials, but it likely isn't too far off, and each of these moments will need the skills and talents of interaction designers to make them easy, fun, and appropriate. How do you change the bathroom mirror from displaying the weather report to displaying e-mail? How do riders leave or see messages left on a bus? The incredible range of design opportunities is apparent.

Frankly, the stakes are simply too high in ubicomp for interaction designers not to be involved. In a typical interaction with a digital device right now, users are in control of the engagement. They determine when the engagement stops and starts. They control how the computer (and through the computer, others) sees and experiences them. Users' bodies, except for their hands and eyes, are for the most part irrelevant. None of this is true in ubicomp.

Users may step into a room and unknowingly begin to engage with a ubicomp system—or many systems. The thermostat, door, light fixture, television, and so on may all be part of different systems, wired to respond to a person's presence. Where users are in the room—even the direction they are facing—may matter. Standing near the television and facing it may trigger it to turn on, as could a particular gesture, such as pretending to click a remote control in the air. But because users may not know any of this, they have no way of controlling how they present themselves to the system. Perhaps they don't want the room to know they are there!

The implications of ubicomp are profound, and it will be up to interaction designers to make these systems discoverable, recoverable, safe, and humane. Like robots, ubicomp systems are often both products and services, so all the skills, methods, and techniques discussed throughout this book (and more) will be needed to design them in a way that works for humans. One can easily imagine how ubicomp systems could get out of control, embarrassing and annoying us. Our privacy could be impinged upon every day, especially since ubicomp is hard to see without signage systems and icons on objects and in areas to let us know we are in a ubicomp environment. We will need to know what is being observed, and how, and where, but hopefully without filling our rooms with signs.

Interaction designers need to design ways for people not only to understand these systems, but also to gain access to them if problems occur. When problems happen—the system switches off the TV every time you sneeze!—how can they be corrected? Is it the lamp that controls the TV or is it the wall?

Adam Greenfield on Everyware

 *Adam Greenfield, author of* Everyware: The Dawning Age of Ubiquitous Computing *(2006), is an internationally recognized writer, user experience consultant, and critical futurist. Before starting his current company, Studies and Observations, he was lead information architect for the Tokyo office of Web consultancy Razorfish; prior to that, he worked as senior information architect for marchFIRST, also in Tokyo. He's also been, at various points in his career, a rock critic for SPIN magazine, a medic at the Berkeley Free Clinic, a coffeehouse owner in West Philadelphia, and a PSYOP sergeant in the U.S. Army's Special Operations Command.*

What do interaction designers need to know about ubiquitous computing, what you call "everyware"?

Probably the single most important thing that we need to wrap our heads around is *multiplicity.*

Instead of the neatly circumscribed space of interaction between a single user and his or her PC, his or her mobile device, we're going to have to contend with a situation in which multiple users are potentially interacting with multiple technical systems in a given space at a given moment.

This has technical implications, of course, in terms of managing computational resources and so on, but for me the most interesting implications concern the quality of user experience. How can we best design informational systems so that they (a) work smoothly in synchrony with *each other*, and (b) deliver optimal experiences to the overburdened human at their focus? This is the challenge that Mark Weiser and John Seely Brown refer to as "encalming, as well as informing," and I think it's one we've only begun to scratch the surface of addressing.

How will the interactions we have with digital products now differ from those in the future?

The simple fact that networked information-processing devices are going to be deployed everywhere in the built environment rather strongly implies the inadequacy of the traditional user interface modalities we've been able to call on, most particularly keyboards and keypads.

When a room, or a lamp post, or a running shoe is, in and of itself, an information gathering, processing, storage, and transmission device, it's crazy to assume that the keyboard or the traditional GUI makes sense as a channel for interaction—somewhat akin to continuing to think of a car as a "horseless carriage." We're going to need to devise ways to interact with artifacts like these that are sensitive to the way we use them, biomechanically, psychologically, and socially. Especially if we want the systems we design to encalm their users, we're going to need to look somewhere else.

Voice and gestural interfaces, in this context, are very appealing candidates, because they so easily accommodate themselves to a wide variety of spaces and contexts, without taking up physical space, or preventing the user from attending to more focal tasks. They become particularly interesting with the expansion in the number of child, elderly, or nonliterate users implied by the increased ambit of post-PC informatics.

You've spoken about "design dissolving into behavior." How can interaction designers accomplish that?

Well, that's a notion of Naoto Fukasawa's, that interactions with designed systems can be so well thought out by their authors, and so effortless on the part of their users, that they effectively abscond from awareness.

Following him, I define everyware at its most refined as "information processing dissolving in behavior." We see this, for example, in Hong Kong, where women leave their RFID-based Octopus cards in their handbags and simply swing their bags across the readers as they move through the turnstiles. There's a very sophisticated transaction between card and reader there, but it takes 0.2 seconds, and it's been subsumed entirely into this very casual, natural, even jaunty gesture.

But that wasn't designed. It just emerged; people figured out how to do that by themselves, without some designer having to instruct them in the nuances. So I'd argue that creating experiences with ubiquitous systems that are of similar quality and elegance is largely a matter of close and careful attention to the way people already use the world. The more we can accommodate and not impose, the more successful our designs will be.

Another challenge when designing for ubicomp is that most ubicomp systems will likely be *stateless*, meaning that they will change from moment to moment—there won't be a place in time (a specific state) that the system can go back to. Users won't be able to refer to an earlier moment and revert to that, or at least not easily, making it harder to undo mistakes—"Wait, what did I just say that caused all the windows of the room to open?" or "Pretend I didn't just walk into this room." Interaction designers will need to take this feature of ubicomp systems into account and design without the benefits of Undo commands and Back buttons.

As with all systems (but, again, more so), it is incumbent upon interaction designers to instill meaning and values into ubicomp. When the things around us are aware, monitoring us and capable of turning our offices, homes, and public spaces into nightmares of reduced civil liberties and insane levels of personalization ("Hi Sarah! Welcome back to the bus! I see you are wearing jeans today. Mind if I show you some ads for Levi's?"), interaction designers need to have compassionate respect for the people who will be engaged with them, some of them unwillingly and unknowingly.

Digital Tools for Making Digital Tools

Forget the future—the present is complicated and sophisticated enough. The skills required to use the technology that is available now are far beyond those of most people. Not only are our devices too difficult to use, tapping into the available technology to do something personal is too challenging. We need tools for making tools.

Humans should be able to design and create applications just for themselves, that fit *their* needs and *their* interests—not just what designers and engineers think they should have. The beauty of Web sites like eBay and MySpace (**Figure 9.9**) is that they allow a person who isn't tech savvy to set up an online business or personal home page or create a social network without knowing anything about how it is done. But now we're at a point where we need a richer set of tools to create richer, individual applications, not just customizable pages.

Some Web sites like Ning (**Figure 9.10**) have taken steps in the right direction, providing all the back-end technology (databases, maps, and so on) necessary for users to create their own Web applications. Where, though, are the tools for doing so on the desktop? On mobile devices? This has been the Holy Grail for years—a simple programming language/toolkit for nonprogrammers—but thus far there has been little progress toward it, perhaps because it has been mainly programmers working on the problem. Tools for programmers have become better, but certainly we are nowhere near the point where someone with little knowledge of technology can put together an application for, say, alerting her when a friend has a new post on his blog.

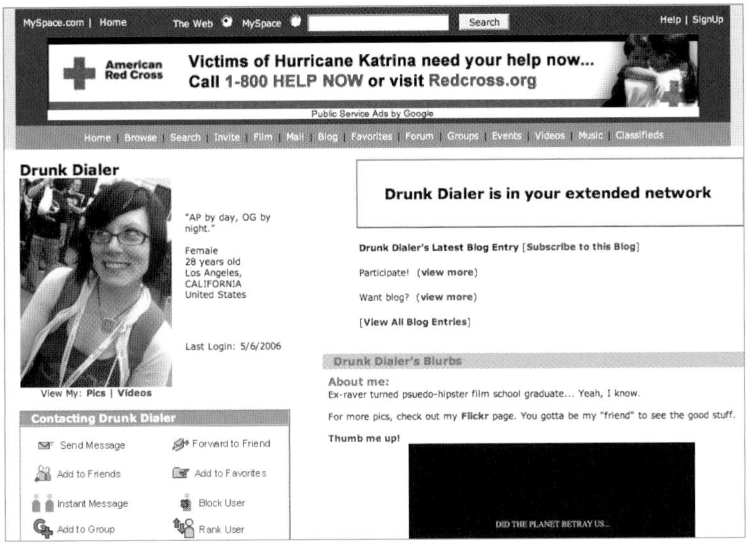

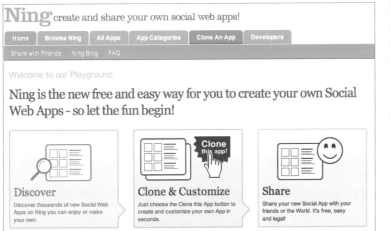

Figure 9.9

MySpace may look unattractive, but it easily allows users to create communities, share music, and post blog entries. It did what many had tried before: lowered the barrier of entry to the creation of personalized home pages.

Figure 9.10

Ning allows users to modify basic types of social networking applications such as reviews and surveys to suit their own needs.

Interaction designers need to find ways to make the already amazing technology we have available *right now* to the billions of people who don't yet have a way to make this technology their own, to create things that, because of their personal nature, have little or no commercial value but great human value. Interaction designers need to make sure that the already wide so-called digital divide between those who have and can use technology and those who thus far cannot gets no wider. Those people—and we are surrounded by them every day—need the tools to make technology relevant to them and their lives.

Summary

"The best way to predict the future," said Alan Kay, the Xerox PARC scientist who came up with the idea of a laptop computer, the Dynabook, in 1972, "is to invent it." The future arrives, second by second, whether we want it to or not, and it is the job of interaction designers to invent it, or at least to make it more humane. The sheer number of products and services, augmented by new technologies, that will become widely available in the next decade and their likely effect on the world will be staggering. Between the advancing technology and the people who will use it stand interaction designers, shaping, guiding, cajoling the future into forms for humans.

Epilogue

Designing for Good

What responsibility do interaction designers have for what they design? Some designers think that the products and services they create are morally neutral, that users themselves and society should determine how a product should be used, not the designer. But what if the user's task is to injure someone? Or if the system being designed helps people do harm?

The book *IBM and the Holocaust* by Edwin Black relates the story of a timber merchant from Bendzin, Poland, who, in August 1943, arrived at the Nazi concentration camp at Auschwitz as a prisoner. There, the Nazis assigned him a five-digit IBM Hollerith number, 44673. This number was later tattooed on his forearm. This number, and thousands like it, were part of a custom punch card system designed by IBM to track prisoners in Nazi concentration camps. (In the IBM system, the Auschwitz camp code was 001.) The Hollerith system tracked prisoners and their availability for work, their punch card numbers following them from labor assignment to labor assignment until most of them were put to death.

The Holocaust was extremely well designed.

When we think of good design, we usually mean products and services that help users complete their tasks in an efficient, effective, aesthetically pleasing manner. That's what the characteristics of good interaction design in Chapter 3 were all about. But there is another definition of "good" that should be considered when designing: the moral, the just, the life affirming—the good that protects human dignity.

Interaction designers should design for this sort of good as well.

Ethics in Design

Any serious examination of interaction design has to include a discussion of ethics. Ethics are what help designers distinguish between good and bad design. Ethics show designers how to respond when asked to do work that is questionable. Ethics are about the consequences of actions; if there were no consequences to interaction design, there'd be no need for ethics. And with the dawning of the age of ubiquitous computing, RFID tags, mobile devices that can track our movements, and robots, wearables, and intelligent agents that have access to our homes and our most private secrets, the consequences for interaction design are more far reaching and more significant than they have ever been.

Ethics are about human decision making: why and how we make the decisions we do. Ethics are about determining what is the *right* thing to do in the given circumstances. Design theorist Richard Buchanan has noted that this is what interaction designers do all the time: determine the right thing to do considering the given constraints. To design is to make ethical choices. In other words, design is ethics in action.

Principles

Being an interaction designer requires principles, because interaction designers help determine what the interactions between people *should* be. Should people be treated with respect? Are some people more deserving of respect than others? Are some people more important than others? Is it okay to make a product good for some people, but less so for others? Should the tools of design even be used on a particular project? These are the types of issues that, knowingly or (usually) unknowingly, interaction designers grapple with all the time, and they require principles on the part of the designer to sort them out.

Principles for interaction designers involve a complex set of guidelines, including the personal beliefs of the designer, the codes of ethics of professional organizations such as the Industrial Designers Society of America (IDSA), and governmental and societal standards for safety and usability. Without a firm set of their own principles, interaction designers can find themselves adopting the beliefs and values of the companies they work for, and this can be a dangerous course, as it was with IBM and Nazi Germany. There needs to be a balance between the ethics of the designers themselves and the ethics of the organizations that employ them.

Deliberate Choices

Interaction designers try to promote certain kinds of interactions between people. Thus, the fundamental ethical baseline for interaction designers should be *the quality of those interactions on both sides of the equation*: the person initiating the interaction (the e-mail sender) and the person receiving it (the e-mail receiver). The content of the communication aside (e-mail spam, say), the quality of those interactions is strongly determined by the decisions the designer makes while designing the product or service. In this context, even the placement of buttons on an interface is an ethical act: Does the designer have respect and compassion for the users? Does this product or service afford the users human dignity? In short, is the design *good*—good for the users, good for those indirectly affected, good for the culture, good for the environment?

The choices interaction designers make need to be deliberate and forward thinking. Designers need to consider the consequences of their design decisions. Designers have a *sacred duty* to the users of their products and services. Every time users perform an action with a designed product or service, they are, indirectly, trusting the designer who created it to have done his or her job, and to have done it ethically. Users trust that not only will the task they want to do be accomplished (an e-mail will get sent and arrive at its destination), but that the product or service (and by extension the designer who designed it) will do no harm. Users entrust designers (through the products and services they design) with intensely personal information—passwords, bank account numbers, credit card numbers, and so on—and, in some cases, with their lives. Designers need to recognize and respect that trust.

It isn't enough, however, to do right by just the individual users. Individual users (and the organizations that may be behind them) may not have the best interests of others at heart. Although, as described in Chapter 7, users will always find ways to use products and services for purposes they weren't designed for, designers need to be cognizant of the potential negative consequences of their designs on those who aren't users or who are forced users— like the timber merchant from Bendzin, Poland, Hollerith number 44673.

But just as there are forces for evil in this world, so there are forces for good. After the carnage and atrocities of World War II, representatives from 50 countries met in April 1945, only a few miles from where I'm writing this in San Francisco, to design a service to humanity, something that would help prevent anything like what happened twice in the 20th century from ever happening again, something that would facilitate and inspire dialogue—interactions—between countries. Their work, their design, became the United Nations. And while the United Nations, like all things made by humans, may be imperfect, its goals of international cooperation, peaceful conflict resolution, human rights, and humanitarian aid, and its actions that support them, are forces for good in the world. May the products and services that interaction designers create all be thus.

Index

Colophon

Designing for Interaction was written and illustrated on an aging titanium Apple PowerBook running Mac OS 10.4. The text was written in Microsoft Word and the figures were created in Adobe InDesign. Photos were manipulated using Adobe Photoshop.

The book was set using Adobe InDesign. Body text is Minion Pro. Headers and most of the figures are Whitney.

The accompanying Web site—designingforinteraction.com—was created using Adobe Dreamweaver and ImageReady, and uses MovableType for content management.